Living in the Heart

Book Design by Paul Ferrini

ISBN # 1-879159-36-8

Manufactured in the United States of America

Living in the Heart

THE AFFINITY PROCESS AND THE PATH OF
UNCONDITIONAL LOVE AND ACCEPTANCE

TABLE OF CONTENTS

PART THREE: PRACTICE —

A MANUAL FOR FACILITATORS

Acknowledgements

I would like to thank the thousands of participants in my conferences, retreats and workshops who have experienced the Affinity Process and given important feedback over the years. I would also like to thank the dedicated people who have been willing to serve others by facilitating this Process in their communities. Please know that your efforts have been greatly appreciated and have helped to bring the Affinity Process to its present stage of development. Through your efforts, and the efforts of people to come, the Affinity Process will do its important work of helping us all rest in our hearts.

To The Reader

The experiential process you will discover in this book has changed the life of thousands of people around the world. It can change your life too if you are willing to practice it. In *A Course in Miracles*, Jesus says that a universal theology is not possible, but a universal experience is. The Affinity Group Process will enable you to have that universal experience of unconditional acceptance and love, which transcends words and thoughts. While religions and philosophies point to this experience, they cannot offer it to you. The Affinity Process can.

The Affinity Process will not eradicate your judgments, but it will help you to sink down through the egoic layers of consciousness from which these judgments arise. You will learn to hold your fears (as well as the fears of others) with such compassion that they no longer have the power to run your life. Instead of blaming others for your pain and your problems, you will learn to take responsibility for what you think, feel, and experience, releasing others to take responsibility for their own lives.

By acknowledging and accepting the aspects of yourself of which you have been afraid or ashamed, you won't need to project them onto others. That means you won't spend your time finding fault with others or trying to fix them. Nor will you feel compelled to give energy to anyone who is judging or trying to fix you. Instead, you will meet others as equals and bring to your relationships the capacity to listen, to accept, and to love without conditions.

The result is freedom from suffering. But this result will not come overnight. The Process revealed in this book requires continual practice. Initially, it requires a commitment of two hours per week. If you can devote yourself to weekly participation in the Process for a year, you will find that a profound shift takes place in your consciousness and your experience. You will begin to internalize the Process and live it in your daily life. You will become the embodiment of love, the living witness to the meeting of self and other in their divine embrace.

Namaste,

Paul Ferrini

Part One: Principles

Living in the Heart

Staying in our hearts is not easy. For it is in the heart that we come to terms with our experience. If our hearts are open, we embrace our experience. We take it in and allow it to integrate in our psyche. If our hearts are closed, we push our experience away. We defend ourselves against disappointment or hurt. We escape into our heads.

The intellectualization of our experience robs us not only of the lows of emotional life, but of the highs as well. We lose the capacity to feel compassion for ourselves and others. We lose our sensitivity not just to pain and suffering, but to beauty and joy as well.

When our hearts are truly open, joy and pain are experienced without story or embellishment. They do not mean anything apart from what they are. Pain doesn't mean that we're bad or that someone else is bad, and joy doesn't mean that we're good. There is no interpretation: just a willingness to embrace and bring the experience in. In the open heart, laughter and tears commingle. It is a place of intense contradiction, a rich place, a multifaceted banquet of experience that cannot be rationalized, tamed, predicted or figured out.

Fear and conditioning encourage us to push away those aspects of our experience that are new, unexpected, or that do not feel safe. By creating an area of our experience that is unacceptable, division is created in the psyche. Now we have good and bad, unconscious and

11

conscious, wanted and unwanted. Now we can have an experience without feeling it. We can escape into our heads, space out, disconnect emotionally. While this kind of dissociation is understandable when it comes in reaction to traumatic events, it is dysfunctional in response to the ups and downs of daily life.

When we are willing to take in only what is familiar to us or what we think we want, we get stuck in the grooves and patterns of our past. We stagnate emotionally and intellectually. We become rigid, ego-centric and pre-dictable. Our life energy gets invested in maintaining our ego-defenses and insuring that the status quo remains intact.

Living in the heart means letting everything in. It means being with our experience, even when it is diffi-cult or confusing. To be in the heart, we often have to postpone making decisions until we have become fully familiar with the whole contents of our consciousness.

Staying in the heart helps us assimilate the vagaries of our experience. Often, it takes time for this to hap-pen. When we take this time, we find that the initial contradictions sort themselves out. Clarity happens as we honor all the different thoughts and feelings in our psyche. It is a function of our felt wholeness.

Deciding something before we have taken this time to be with all of our contradictory thoughts and feelings often exacerbates whatever conflict we are experiencing in our outer lives. When we feel an urgency or pressure to decide or figure things out, it usually means that we are escaping into our heads, trying to "make something happen" that is not ready to happen. And this inevitably leads to outward struggle and disappointment. The doors do not open, no matter how hard or how frequently we knock on them. Because we are not in inner harmony, we cannot be in harmony with others. Because we are not in our own "flow," we cannot flow with life as it manifests around us.

It takes courage to be present in our inner emotional landscape when rain or fog obscure the long view. When visibility is at a minimum, all we can do is put one foot in front of the other. When lots of conflicting thoughts and emotions are churning in the psyche, all we can do is bring our awareness gently to where we are. If we rush through the rain or the fog, we will stray from the path and fall. An accident will delay us from our goal much longer than bad weather will, and then, we will wish that we had been more patient.

To be patient with ourselves and our own process is the key to living in the heart. We can be in our hearts and not "know" the outcome of a situation. Indeed, the willingness "to be without knowing" is essential to being present here and now for whatever we are experiencing. "Knowing" is almost always about the past. When we no longer have to know, we can stay in this moment.

The Present Moment

In our society, doing is prized more than being. Our self image is built more on what we do than on who we are. When we are concerned with doing and getting things done, we tend to live in the past or the future. Sometimes, that is inevitable. But if we spend most of our time in this space, we will experience very little peace.

Peace comes when we can take a deep breath and just be present right now. Peace comes when we realize that we do not have to bring our past fears into this moment, nor do we have to make decisions about the future. Peace is always present-oriented. Peace comes when we can stay in our hearts without having "to know" or "to do."

Without the pressure "to know" or "to do," life is much more simple. It is easier to accept and assimilate the experience that comes our way. We don't have to resist what happens or defend ourselves against it. We don't have to intellectualize it or figure it out. We don't have to know what it means. We can just dwell with it, let it be, let it come in.

Living in the heart is a very different way of living than we are used to. It is a slower, simpler pace. When we think, we are practical in our thinking. We are concrete, down to earth. Abstract thinking has very little place in our life, because it takes us away from this moment. In the same way, when we act, we do so without ambivalence or deliberation. We don't blindly follow a set of rules. We act because it feels right to act in that moment.

There is no complexity of mind in this way of being. There is no great drama, no scheming and dreaming, no perfectionism or second guessing. We put our best foot forward and we trust. We know that any more than this is just not possible. Doing the best that we can in the moment is and has to be enough.

That doesn't mean that we don't make mistakes. Of course we make mistakes, but these mistakes are not our enemies; they are our friends. They help us to find correction. They empower us to do better the next time. We don't feel guilty and hide our faces when we err. We don't feel shamed or rejected. We stand up and say "thank you for telling me."

An empowered person does not feel shamed by his own mistakes, nor does he feel superior to others when they make mistakes. He accepts himself as he is in this moment. He accepts others as they are.

Sanity comes from living simply with dignity. It comes from respecting oneself and others. It comes from staying in the present moment. It comes from staying in the heart when life shows up differently than we expect it to.

Not Fixing

When we stay in the heart, we know that there is no one to fix. We don't have to fix other people. We don't have to fix ourselves.

To live in the heart, we must drop our self-help programs, and just focus on accepting ourselves as we are in this moment. To live in the heart, we must drop our missionary programs and just focus on accepting others as they are in this moment. Programs for the improvement, salvation, redemption of self or other are just diversions that take us away from the real spiritual work of practicing acceptance moment to moment.

If people want to take a trip, they are free to. We don't have to interfere or try to dissuade them. We don't have to try to fix them with our teaching of "not fixing." Any teaching can become a stick that we use to beat up ourselves or others. That's why we need to stay away from dogma.

If we want to stay in the heart, we need to stay out of dogma. We need to burn our scrolls, our commandments, our holy books. They are distractions too. Anything or anyone that tells us what to do, or what to say, or what to think must go. To be in the heart, we must clear the mind of the judgments and prejudices of the past. The more open our minds are, the easier it becomes to fall into the heart.

To be in the heart, we can have only one authority. And that authority cannot be outside us, vested in the ideas, beliefs or experiences of others, nor can it be inside our ego structure, vested in the limited ideas or beliefs we have about ourselves. It must be inside our minds, but outside our judgments and narrow beliefs. It must be inside our hearts, but outside our reactive emotions and addictions. We can't submit to someone else's truth. Nor can we submit to the limited "truth" of our ego.

The kingdom of heaven is within our hearts, but that does not mean it is easy to discover. First, we have to accept everything that is happening in our experience. We have to accept our relationships just the way they are. We have to accept all our thoughts and feelings. We have to let it all in, get our arms around it, however tentatively. We have to live with it, be with it, breathe with it, move with it, and shift with it as it shifts.

It requires all our presence, all our attention, all our patience, all our gentleness. And when we have given all of this, there is a clear space that opens in the heart. There is a silence. And into that space and that silence the answer we need rushes in, like air into a vacuum. It may not be the ultimate answer, but it is the answer for right now. It shows us the way to proceed, to take the next step.

And the answer that enters the silence of the heart is the movement of Spirit into our lives. Lest we hold the space open, Spirit's answer cannot come.

When we get quiet, we understand that Spirit's answer does not come from our limited, fearful, ego-mind, but from the mind of God, from the part of us that is joined with love and is not invested in our drama of pain and suffering. So we wait. We lay aside our one-sided solution and await the solution that honors all beings. We submit to the One who knows, who is in us, yet outside our narrowness. We wait for the Christ consciousness to be born within our hearts and minds.

Holding the Space

In the Affinity Process we call this "holding the space" of unconditional love and acceptance. We do this by being gentle with ourselves and others, by accepting and respecting our experience exactly as it is here and now.

Holding the space is not as easy as it sounds. It is a tremendous challenge, because it is so different from anything we have been taught to do.

When I hold the space for myself, I get quiet and become aware of what I am thinking and how I am feeling. I also become aware of any judgments I have about what's happening. For example, I hear the critical voice within me that says "If you were more spiritual, you wouldn't be angry."

I allow all the voices in my psyche to speak to me and I accept them into my awareness. I do not make them good or bad. I just recognize that they are there. No matter how many layers of self-judgment come up, I take them all in.

In my awareness, I am the witness of my experience, not the judge or the jury. As the witness, I do not know what any of it means, nor do I need to know. As the witness, I do not have to do anything about the situation. Instead, I become aware of everything I would like to do to change the situation, but I don't feel any pressure to act. I just notice my dissatisfaction, my need to fix, without judging it. As the witness, my awareness is enough. And it is all that is asked for.

Deepening in my awareness of the contents of my consciousness in this moment, I become still. I sink down through all the layers of judgmental thought and reactive feeling until I realize in both mind and heart that everything is okay exactly as it is. This is the place of self-blessing, the place where I reconnect to love.

Releasing Others

One of the biggest impediments to finding the place of self-blessing is our need to blame other people for our thoughts, feelings or experiences. The wounded little kid in you and me wants to say to the other person "You made me angry. It's your fault that I'm upset."

When we blame others, we try to push the responsibility for our experience onto someone else. Blaming others is our way of denying our responsibility for our unloving thoughts, feelings and actions ("It's not my fault that I'm angry"). It is also our way of justifying our trespasses ("I have a right to be angry"), instead of admitting them and atoning for them.

We cannot hold the space for ourselves as long as we are blaming other people. As we get quiet, it is important for us to become aware of all of the ways that we want to blame other people. As the witness, we see our need to blame without identifying with it. We just notice all the anger and woundedness inside. We notice the desire to strike back and punish others for our suffering. We go through those layers of shame and blame until we come to a place that is empty. In that place, we can face how we feel directly, without making anyone else responsible for it. In that place, we can release others, and be with our feelings compassionately.

Non-judgmental Awareness

The goal in all of this is to encounter the contents of our consciousness without judging them, to cultivate compassion first for ourselves and then for others. The irony, of course, is that as soon as we desire to love and accept unconditionally, we immediately become aware of our judgments.

Nowhere is this more apparent than in our relationships with others. While our self-judgments are often hidden in our psyche, our judgments of other people are constantly visible on the surface. Just in the course of a single day, we have hundreds of judgments. We don't like how loudly this person talks. We don't like his table manners. We don't like the way she wears her hair. And so forth.

Our judgments are so commonplace that we are rarely aware of them. We're on automatic pilot.

To live in the heart, we don't have to stop our steady stream of judgments about others; we just need to become aware of them. Awareness allows us to go deeper.

Taking Responsibility

The more aware we become of our judgments, the more we realize that they really don't have very much to do with the people we are judging. Rather, they have a lot to do with how we feel about ourselves.

It is not the object of our ridicule that tells us something, but the consciousness in which that ridicule originates. The mind that judges others does not have a very high opinion of self. Rather than face that lack of self-esteem directly, we project it onto others.

As we practice awareness, we begin to see that we judge only when we are not feeling good about ourselves and/or when someone reminds us of some part of ourselves we have trouble accepting. In this manner, we begin to "own" our judgments, instead of projecting them. As each judgment comes up, we say "I know that this is not about you; it is about me."

We take responsibility for the contents of our consciousness. We take others off the hook.

Now we are able to deal directly with the phenomenon of our self-hatred. Now we can see intimately which parts of ourselves we can't accept. Other people are just mirrors that help us see how we judge ourselves.

By acknowledging that our judgment originates in

our consciousness, we see that there is a part of ourselves that does not feel loved and accepted. That part of us judges other people and perhaps, more importantly, that part of us feels judged. It may be the spiritual adult judging the wounded child or it may be the wounded child judging the spiritual adult. It doesn't matter. If there is judgment happening, there is separation, conflict, within our consciousness.

Some part of us is in conflict with another part of us. Acceptance is needed to create the conditions for reconciliation of this conflict within our own consciousness.

Acceptance

When I am judging myself, I am not feeling whole. I am feeling conflicted or divided. Different aspects of my self are in conflict and must be accepted as they are. When I accept, I don't resolve the conflict. I just see it and acknowledge it.

Here is an example. Let's say I judge John for being angry, because I think being angry is bad. As I look at why John's anger triggered me, I see that there is a part of me that is angry and needs to be acknowledged. I also see that I am afraid of/ashamed of my anger. As a result, I repress or disguise it.

When John is angry in an all-out, undisguised way, I get upset, because he is doing what I would like to do but will not allow myself to do. When I see John's anger, my uneasy relationship to my own anger is triggered.

Now, thanks to John, I can begin to look at my relationship to my own anger. I can accept the part of me that wants to get angry and stand up for myself, as well as the part of me that is afraid to get angry because I want to please others. I acknowledge these seemingly opposing aspects of my own consciousness.

Now this does not immediately heal the rift within. It simply places my compassionate awareness there. And that, in itself, is healing. That, in itself, is a bringing of love.

Living Our Awareness

Now I am aware of what my inner conflict is. So the next time someone gets angry and my buttons are pushed, I am going to acknowledge first to myself and then to the other person that I am angry and it is not easy for me to express my anger. I might say to the other person something like: "I'm very angry at you right now, but I'm afraid to express my anger, because I think that if I do you'll leave me." I state the truth of my experience, however conflicted it may be. I learn to stand up for myself in a way that does not terrify me. The key is that I need to honor all of myself.

Living my awareness means making room in my life for all of me to be present: the part of me that is afraid and the part that is confident, the part that wants self-expression and the part that wants approval or acceptance. By allowing all of me to be visible to myself and others, I have less chance of feeling betrayed or misunderstood.

My awareness of, responsibility for, and acceptance of my judgments help me to be more honest with myself and more present with others. I take small steps into greater authenticity, and as I do, I find it easier to accept others as they are.

After all, every fault I find with another is a grievance I have against myself. Every fight I pick with my brother or sister underscores the conflict I have within myself. I cannot make peace with others until I become aware of its source within myself. Then, and then alone, can I begin the work of inner and outer reconciliation.

The Work of Reconciliation

As we practice being aware of our judgments, seeing where they originate, taking responsibility for them, and accepting all the unloved and conflicted aspects of our consciousness, we gradually stop externalizing our pain and begin to heal it internally.

These understandings are essential for our release from pain and conflict and our ongoing healing:

- Each of us is responsible for everything we think, feel, and experience.

- Every judgment we have about someone else shows us some aspect of ourselves we have not learned to accept and love.

🦢 It is our responsibility to accept and love all aspects of ourselves, especially the parts of us that feel unloved and unlovable.

If we can live these simple understandings on an ongoing basis, we can come into more loving relationship with ourselves and others. But living them requires practice. And practice is called for not just when we are coasting through life and feeling spiritual, but when life is showing up differently than the way we expect it to and our buttons are being pushed.

Here are two simple guidelines for ongoing practice of staying in the heart:

🦢 When we are confused, upset or reactive in relationship to others, hold a space of unconditional love and acceptance for ourselves so that we can begin to take responsibility for our experience.

🦢 When others are confused, upset or reactive in relationship to us, support them in taking responsibility for their experience by holding a space of unconditional love and acceptance for them.

This practice is not very difficult to understand. We don't have to be geniuses to know what we are being asked to do. Yet if you try practicing these two guidelines, you will find that they are very challenging. It's not easy to hold a space for yourself when you are upset, nor is it easy to hold a space for others when they are reactive.

Nobody said it would be easy. Simple, yes. But not easy!

That's why we designed the Affinity Process . . . to help you practice . . . not with your spouse, your parent, your child, your boss—the people who really push your buttons—but with people you don't know who, like you, have the willingness to begin to look at their judgments. We wanted to make it as easy as possible for you to learn this simple, but challenging process of living in the heart.

We figured that once you had gotten the hang of practicing with strangers, you could take the practice home. Then when your partner yells at you and gets in your face, you would know what to do, right? Well, maybe not right away. But you would have some tools to use when little disagreements come up and threaten to escalate.

Because you have some degree of skillfulness in holding a safe space for yourself and others, you can weather the small storms in your relationships. And you and your family/friends can begin to build sufficient trust to take on the typhoons that arise unexpectedly on the ocean of life.

Origins of the Affinity Process

The Affinity Process was developed to help us move through our conflicts without destroying the love that we feel for each other. Several years ago, I began running conferences for students of *A Course in Miracles*. Often we would bring together 200–300 people. We would sing, dance, eat together, play together. Many of us experienced an intimacy with people we had just met that we had not experienced before in our lives, even with family, spouses and friends. When we were willing to trust and accept one another, our experience was one of giving and receiving love. It was ecstatic. Then, we would go home and get back into our old stories and defense mechanisms and our emotional bubbles would burst. We would go from feeling joyful, trusting, and expansive to feeling sad, defensive, and emotionally contracted. We couldn't bring the trust and the acceptance home with us. As soon as our buttons were pushed by parents, children, friends, or lovers, we were back to living in fear. We simply did not have the tools we needed to process our egoic material.

In any relationship, no matter how good or trusting it is at first, our ego issues are bound to surface. When we start feeling safe with a person, our subconscious fears begin to come up for healing. When one person is in the grip of fear, it doesn't take long before the other reacts in fear too. Indeed, fear is contagious. If you don't know how to love yourself unconditionally, you don't have much chance of not reacting to someone else's distancing or attacking behavior.

When we are scared, we either try to take control or we run away. Fight or flight is the norm.

Rarely do we hang in there, recognize that we have fear coming up and take responsibility for it. How often do we say to our partner: "I have a lot of fear coming up which you seemed to trigger, but I know it's my fear and I need some time to deal with it. If I try to talk to you about it now, I'll make it about you, not me, and I don't want to do that. I want to feel it, own it, understand it and then come back and talk to you about it when I am ready."

Usually, when our fear comes up, we get defensive or we run away. Either way, we want to make it the other person's problem. The other person, in turn, wants to make his or her fear our problem. The result is that we both feel separation. We both feel attacked.

No matter how hard we try, we are not going to get rid of our ego material. It's going to come up. Today, we might accept each other and see eye to eye. But, tomorrow we might not agree. Tomorrow, we might not feel supported by each other. And in the face of disagreement and lack of support, will we still accept each other?

Most of our love is conditional. We love each other when we agree and feel mutually supported. When agreement and support ends, love generally gets cut off.

Jesus told us to "love our enemies." He might as well have said "love your friends and lovers when they stop being supportive to you." It's the same challenge. Can we love and respect people who disagree with us? Can we love people who have judgments about us?

When fear comes up in our relationship, can we love each other through the fear? Or does love disappear as soon as our fears arise?

Successful relationships are those in which love survives the onslaught of fear. They take time to develop. Superficial trust is not enough. Deep childhood fears will easily overwhelm it. Trust must go deeper than our fear, or our partner's fear.

Holding Our Fear With Compassion

The truth is that if we can learn to be with our own fear in a loving and compassionate way, it is easier to deal with the fear of others. So part of the challenge is entirely personal. We need to learn to love ourselves when our fear comes up.

That means that we acknowledge our fear and refuse to project it onto another person. And this is where the Affinity Process begins.

When I'm doing the Affinity Process and I have a judgment about you, I know that judgment comes from my own fear. I own that fear and take responsibility for loving myself through that moment of fear, instead of verbally attacking you.

The Affinity Process makes me responsible for everything that I am thinking or feeling. If I am sad or angry, the sadness and anger belong to me. Even if you appeared to provoke these emotions in me, they are not your responsibility.

By insisting that each person take responsibility for what s/he is thinking or feeling, the Process prevents fear from escalating. It calls a truce in the midst of the conflict and gives each side homework to do.

My homework is always to be with my fear when it comes up. Your homework is to be with your fear. When you focus on what I do or say, you can't be with your fear. When I focus on your behavior or your words, I can't be with my fear.

You may have triggered my fear, but you are not the cause of it. The dynamite was already there waiting to be lit. Even the matches were there. Anyone could have come along and lit a match. It just happened to be you.

When I take you off the hook and face my fear directly, I learn how to love myself unconditionally. I learn to deal compassionately with my own feelings of unworthiness. I stop looking to you to supply the love I'm lacking and learn to supply it myself.

When I am actively loving myself, then I am strong enough to love you through our disagreement. I am strong enough to support myself when you cannot support me.

The more loving I become toward myself, the easier it is for me to be with people who judge me, criticize me, or attack me. I know that I am not responsible for how they think or feel about me; I am responsible only for what I think and feel, about myself and about them.

My love for myself and others is no longer dependent on agreement or support. To be sure, I enjoy agreement and support, but I won't stop loving when they are not offered. Indeed, those are the times when I need to love myself and others more.

Opening Our Hearts

The Affinity Process helps us to be with our fear and move through it. Instead of projecting our fear onto others, we take responsibility for it and learn to bring love to the hurt places in ourselves.

Due to past trauma, our hearts are defended. We are suspicious of people, not just people who are mean to us, but also people who really care about us. We are afraid they too will attack us or abandon us.

Trusting others is a big issue for us. Yet we know that it is only through trust that we can experience the fulfillment our relationships promise.

In the past, we justified our lack of trust by maintaining that others did not deserve our trust. But the Affinity Process asks us to be responsible for all of our experience, including our experience of not trusting.

So now I can't say I'm not trusting because of something that you did or said. You may have triggered my lack of trust. But you are not responsible for it.

I have my own reasons for not trusting that have nothing to do with you. In fact, it may not be you that I don't trust. It might be me.

Anyway, trust is my issue. My heart is the one that's closed. I am the one who is pushing away love. I am the one who is suffering.

If I want my heart to open, I must be willing to trust myself. I don't have to start with big things. I can start to trust in little ways.

I see what I like and give myself permission to have it. I trust that I know what's good for me, even if it isn't what others want. I move toward my joy and my happiness. I don't question them.

When I begin to trust myself, even in little ways, I am drawn to people who are learning to trust themselves too. Friendships become more fulfilling. Partnerships become less sacrificial.

When I'm trusting myself, I'm no longer living out the unconscious myth that I'm not trustworthy. I'm no longer projecting my fears onto another person. I'm not attracting a partner who mirrors my lack of trust in myself.

No, instead I'm consciously working with my trust issue. I'm learning to trust myself in small ways. I'm building a consciousness of self-trust and, as I do, I'm demonstrating that in all areas of my life.

When we stop projecting, we can acknowledge our weaknesses and work on them without feeling shame. We can see our mistakes compassionately and learn from them. We don't need to blame others. We don't need to feel guilty and blame ourselves. We can move on, become more conscious, and awaken from our unconscious patterns of self-denial.

It is one of the ironies of relationship that no one else can open our hearts. We may have closed our hearts down to protect ourselves from others, but the truth is that we are the ones locked into our closed hearts. We are the ones who suffer from lack of trust and lack of freedom.

We are the ones who must open our hearts, but we won't do so until we feel safe. We need to be able to create safety for ourselves. We need to be able to create safety with others.

The Affinity Process helps us do that by offering us clear guidelines for creating an environment of unconditional love and acceptance for ourselves and others. And, in this environment, the muscles of our heart, long contracted and fearful, can begin to open once again.

Part Two: Process

What Our Affinity Is

We call this the Affinity Process because the word affinity suggests a "community of interest" amongst people who see each other as equals and have each other's highest good at heart. Our "affinity" is our common humanness and our mutual desire to love and be loved.

Our affinity is not based on having the same culture, experience, or a common set of beliefs, but on our willingness to respect each other's culture, experience and beliefs. Our affinity does not consist of our agreement, but our willingness to honor our differences. In the Affinity Process, we learn to trust that others will hear us and respect us when we tell our truth, and we learn to listen respectfully when others tell us their truth.

The Affinity Process helps us become aware of and take responsibility for our judgments, instead of projecting them onto others. It helps us learn to hold a loving, compassionate space for ourselves in which we can come to greater acceptance of all parts of ourselves. It helps us place our loving awareness on the unloved parts of ourselves so that we can bring healing and wholeness to our psyche. It empowers us to become more loving, more authentic beings.

The Affinity Process also helps us learn how to listen to others without judgment. It teaches us how to create a safe, loving space, where others can take responsibility for their own judgments and connect with their own compassion, love and capacity for healing. It is as empowering to others as it is to us.

The Affinity Process is about opening to the Spirit at the deepest level of our being. It is about peeling away the layers of judgment, shame and fear which appear to separate us from God within ourselves and within each other. It is about connecting with our innocence, our spiritual essence, our capacity to accept and bless our own experience and that of others.

It is about moving through our fears to reclaim the love that has never left us. It is about moving from distrust to trust, from shame to self-disclosure, from betrayal to trust in self and others.

It is amazing that so much healing can happen from a simple practice of awareness, responsibility and acceptance. But those who have experienced the process are witnesses to this fact. They have learned a new more compassionate relationship to themselves and others. They have turned their judgments into blessings, their swords into plowshares.

Confession and Purification

In the Affinity Process, we not only become aware of our judgments and learn to take responsibility for them, we also verbalize our self-judgments, fears and feelings of discomfort. This verbalization is an important step in the overall process of coming to acceptance of ourselves and others.

When I realize that my judgment of you is just a mask for my self-judgment, I can tell you honestly that I was judging you but realized that you just reminded me of some part of me I don't like. And then I can talk about my own shame. I can get those uncomfortable feelings up on the table, instead of hiding them inside.

The Affinity Process encourages people to stop projecting, to stop hiding behind the mask of judgment, and to begin to come to grips with their own doubt, fear and guilt. When it works best, members feel safe in expressing thoughts and feelings which are heavy on their hearts. They can do this because they know that no one is going to interrupt them or try to fix them.

This closely parallels the kinds of confession rituals experienced by members of the early Christian communities. They too created a safe, non-judgmental space where members could express their fears and regrets, and reconnect with the loving Spirit of God. There, as in the Affinity Group, psycho-emotional purification took place on a weekly basis, helping community members return to their lives with a renewed consciousness of their innate innocence and worthiness.

Large temples and churches simply cannot offer this kind of intimate purification ritual as part of their worship services. Often, the focus is on performing and putting on a good show for the congregation. Members do not have the opportunity to participate in a heart-felt way in the service. As a result, their fears and judgments remain hidden and, after the entertainment value of the weekly service wears off, they once again experience their pain, alienation and self-hatred. People can hide their pain in a large congregation, but they cannot hide it in an Affinity Group.

While hard and fast rules are rarely helpful, it seems that full-participation in the sacred space of Sabbath requires smaller groups of people. Realizing this, some churches and temples are offering Affinity Groups as a way to build intimacy and connection within the larger community. This helps to meet the needs of individual members for an ongoing transformational experience.

Extending Love to Others

Affinity groups are offered free of charge to anyone who wants to participate and is willing to commit to follow the guidelines. We consider these groups to be a spiritual practice which should be available to all people regardless of their ability to pay. By not asking for an exchange of money, we insure that the process is open to everyone.

In lieu of an exchange of money, we ask members who feel they have been helped by the Process to offer it to others. Once they complete the process, we support members in facilitating or co-facilitating the process with a new group. We ask members to consider some area of their lives in which the process might be a valuable service. For example, one member might be guided to offer the Process in a school to teenagers. Another might offer it in a prison or in a cancer treatment program in a hospital. There is no environment where sacred space cannot be created using the Affinity Process.

Through this process of extension, a safe, loving, non-judgmental space can be created on a community-wide basis. By reaching out to people in all economic and social groups through the Affinity Process, a group or organization can become identified in its town or city as a source of inspiration, hope and loving service.

The Affinity Process helps people from different backgrounds hear, understand, and respect each other on a deeper level. Using the Affinity Process, new relationships are possible between people of different religions, races, and economic or political backgrounds.

As such, the Process becomes a living spiritual community, an interfaith church without walls whose essential purpose is to experience love and extend it. Such a community is open to all and invites the full experiential participation of all of its members.

A Practical, Experiential Process

This process will not appeal to those who are interested in abstract concepts or in spirituality as an intellectual disciple. The Affinity Process is simple and hands-on. It helps us stay in our hearts. It helps us stay in the present moment.

There is nothing elite or esoteric about the Process. It has a set of guidelines (described in depth later). Anyone who is willing to accept those guidelines can be a participant. There are no other prerequisites.

The Process is experiential. Participants learn from practice. As such, the Process requires a commitment of time and attention.

Time Commitment

The first commitment is to meet with a group once per week for eight to ten weeks to learn the Process. Then, if the Process has been helpful, a second commitment of eight to ten weeks is requested. During this second commitment, members agree to extend the process to others by facilitating or co-facilitating a group.

After members have fulfilled these two commitments, some may decide to move onto other things. If so, we hope that they will continue to use the Affinity Process on an informal basis in their relationships with people. Other members may want to continue to facilitate groups so that they stay current with their own weekly spiritual practice and make the Process available to others who hear about it and wish to participate in a group.

Like anything, the Affinity Process must be practiced if it is to be mastered. If you find that it continues to be helpful to you after working with it for four months, you may want to adopt it as your ongoing spiritual practice. People who decide to do this are offered opportunities to participate in Affinity Retreats and work toward becoming Affinity Coordinators.

Once you have really internalized the Affinity Group Guidelines, your entire relationship to yourself and others will be transformed. And you will bring the insights you gained in this Process into every area of your life.

Starting a Group

Ideally, an Affinity Group would have a minimum of six and a maximum of twelve people. Eight people plus a facilitator is the perfect size. With this size, each individual has plenty of opportunity to practice listening, as well as the chance to share significantly during each session.

It is helpful if the group is somewhat diverse, containing both men and women of different ages and backgrounds. We discourage couples and close friends from being in the same Affinity Group. They already have patterns of interaction which may too easily compromise their ability to work within the Affinity Guidelines. By placing close friends or partners in different groups, the process is spared dealing with partnership issues that are more appropriately resolved on a one-to-one basis or with a therapist.

When beginning a group, we suggest keeping it simple. An optimal group is composed of people who do not know each other or know each other just casually. That way, participants can practice the process safely in the present moment.

These are just suggestions. If you want to start a group, you must decide for yourself how you want to proceed. Remember, an Affinity Group happens when all members of the group agree to practice the guidelines. That is the only rule that must be observed.

We suggest that each group meet once per week for eight to ten weeks. We ask that members make a commitment to attend all sessions, baring an emergency. To help people understand just what they are committing to, it is often helpful to have a guest evening, during which potential participants can ask questions about the process or do a dry-run through it. Also, at this time, people who have experienced the process can share what it has meant to them.

Since socializing is not encouraged during or immediately after group sessions, we suggest that the eight week sessions conclude with a pot luck celebration where people can socialize freely and give feedback on what the process has meant to them. This is also a time when future opportunities to participate in and extend the Affinity Process can be discussed.

The Nature of Sharing in a Group

Members of an Affinity Group share what they are thinking and feeling in the moment. Sharing is voluntary, but not required. It is important that each person feel free to participate as s/he is inclined to do so in the moment.

We suggest that members share from their hearts about any matter which is causing them discomfort. If they are feeling anger, guilt, pain, grief, or any other emotional contraction, we encourage them to verbalize how they are feeling without going into a long, complicated story. We also encourage people to verbalize any judgments they are having about their situation which may be exacerbating their pain.

We ask people to try to stay in the present moment and say what they are thinking and feeling right now. That keeps things focused and helps people stay away from telling every detail of their situation in a way that strains the group's attention. Most sharings last five or ten minutes, although shorter or longer sharings may occasionally be appropriate.

People are encouraged to express positive feelings too when that is what their experience is. But they are discouraged from pretending to be happy when they are secretly running judgments about themselves or others in the group.

The goal is to allow everyone who wants to an opportunity to share. But realistically, one person may have little or nothing to share during one session and a lot to share during another session, depending on what is happening in his or her life.

Each sharing is unconditionally accepted and honored by the group. No one tries to fix or give advice to anyone who has shared.

The Affinity Group Process: Purpose, Guidelines, and Agreements

THE PURPOSE OF THE GROUP

The purpose of the Affinity Group Process is to give and receive unconditional love, acceptance and support; to create a safe, loving, non-judgmental space in which we can open our hearts and move through our fears.

THE GROUP GUIDELINES

1. Remember our Purpose: We are here to love and accept one another, not to judge, analyze, rescue or try to fix one another.

2. We agree to share from our hearts and be honest about what we are thinking and feeling.

3. When our Judgments come up about someone, we will be aware of them and gently bring our attention back to the person speaking.

4. We will not interrupt anyone's process. We will give the person sharing our undivided attention. We will not engage in cross-talk.

5. We will take thirty seconds in silence to acknowledge each person's sharing.

6. We will not monopolize the group's time and attention. We will yield the floor to others in the group who have shared less than we have.

7. We will make "I" Statements, not "You" statements. We will take responsibility for our own experiences and respect the experience of others. We will not assign "our" meaning to something someone else has said.

8. We will not hide our hurt or angry feelings. We will share them honestly, without trying to make others responsible for how we feel.

9. If someone shares a hurt or angry feeling with us, we will acknowledge how s/he feels. We will not defend ourselves or try to justify our words or actions. We will share any feelings that come up for us.

10. We will stay in the present moment. We will not bring up the past or future, unless they are happening for us here and now.

11. We will keep everything that is said in the group confidential.

12. We will honor the silence, knowing that it offers us an opportunity to become more deeply present to ourselves and others.

13. If we feel that the group is going "off-purpose," we will ask for a moment of silence, during which our group can re-center and remember its purpose.

14. Remembering that we won't do this process perfectly, we will be gentle with ourselves. We will use whatever transpires in the group as an opportunity to practice forgiveness.

AGREEMENTS

1. We agree to honor the purpose of the group.

2. We agree to practice the guidelines.

3. We agree to be on time for every group meeting.

4. We agree to attend every meeting of the group.

Commentary on the Purpose of the Group

The purpose of the Affinity Group Process is to give and receive unconditional love, acceptance and support, to create a safe, loving, non-judgmental space in which we can open our hearts and move through our fears.

The Affinity Group Process offers us a spiritual practice. Because it meets once per week it offers us a way of observing and honoring the Sabbath, even if we don't feel comfortable attending a church or synagogue.

The Sabbath is a time when we come together on a regular basis to remember God. It is a day that we set aside for rest, fellowship, and connection with Spirit. It is a day when we voluntarily give up our focus on the affairs of the world and remember the purpose of our incarnation. We do this in community with others to support each other in remembering.

The Sabbath is God's day. Affinity Group meetings are God's time. They are sacred space. This is true regardless of the setting in which the group meets. Whether it meets in a business setting, a prison, a cancer treatment center, an elementary school, a homeless shelter, a church, or a private home, the Affinity group is sacred space and time. It is a place where we can come to feel safe and to hold a safe space for others.

The Affinity Group can happen in any environment with any group of people. Leaders of countries in conflict can learn to communicate through the Affinity

Process. Employees and managers can develop greater sensitivity to each other. Children can learn to take responsibility for themselves and respect each other's experience.

The purpose is simple and broad for this reason. The Affinity Process can be experienced by anyone who is willing to practice the guidelines.

The Affinity Group Process is not outcome-oriented. The group does not try to solve problems or reach consensus. It may lead to clarity and consensus, but this is not its purpose. Its purpose is to provide each person with an experience of giving and receiving unconditional love and support.

Better understanding, more compassion, increased respect, better communication are all natural outcomes of the Affinity Process. Individual members learn how to take more responsibility for their thoughts, feelings and experiences; they also learn to refrain from taking inappropriate responsibility for the thoughts, feelings and experiences of others. The Affinity Process helps people develop a healthy sense of boundaries.

The Affinity Process is also an At-one-ment Process. It provides us with a safe place to express our confusion, our pain, our remorse and our judgments so that they are not buried inside us. Because nobody tries to fix us, we learn to hold our own sharing with acceptance and compassion.

The greatest gift of the Affinity Process is self-acceptance. As we learn to accept all the dichotomous aspects of self, we experience greater wholeness, greater confidence, greater creative freedom. With self-acceptance also comes the capacity to accept others as they are, to respect their experience, and to encourage them to be honest and authentic.

Commentary on the Guidelines

1. *Remember our Purpose: We are here to love and accept one another, not to judge, analyze, rescue or try to fix one another.*

Our Purpose is important. It is what distinguishes this group from many other groups which encourage us to share our thoughts and feelings. In an Affinity group, we keep the space safe and loving by refraining from actions which interrupt people's process or show a lack of respect for it. We don't try to fix others, because we believe in the deepest sense that others are okay just the way they are. They may not believe that they are okay, but we believe it and hold that belief for them, no matter how much they may belittle themselves or ask for our advice.

In an Affinity Group, we are not here to agree or disagree with others, but to witness to their sharing, to be as fully present as we can be. The more we judge what they are saying or how they are saying it, the more contracted we become and the less present we are able to be.

Of course, as in any group, we will forget our purpose. That is why this is the most important guideline. When we remember our purpose, we will think, feel and act in ways that are consistent with it.

During the course of a single group session, we will have to remember our purpose thirty, forty or fifty times. That is part of the discipline of the work.

2. *We agree to share from our hearts and be honest about what we are thinking and feeling.*

Being honest about our experience is essential for authentic sharing. If we are feeling peaceful, then it is fine to communicate this. But if we say we are feeling peaceful when we are having judgments, feeling separate from someone in the group, or wondering if the group is right for us, then we aren't being honest. We aren't using the opportunity the group provides us with to honestly express our experience. By holding back the truth, we also hold our feelings inside, where they become heavy on our hearts.

When we tell the truth, we let the things which trouble us come out into the light of day, knowing that others will hold our communication with acceptance and compassion. Even if we are having judgments about others in the group, we can acknowledge these judgments to ourselves, own them, and then talk about them when it is our time to share.

Sharing from the heart is not easy for many of us. When we aren't sure what we are feeling, sometimes it helps to close our eyes, breathe, and tune into our body sensations. Our awareness of the tightness in our shoulders, for example, might remind us of an interaction that took place in the office earlier in the day. We can begin to be aware that the interaction may not be resolved, because we are still carrying it around in our body. This may help us get in touch with some anger or guilt which we could share with the group.

Tuning into body sensations enables us to shift our focus from the head, where we tend to intellectualize our feelings, to the heart, where we can experience our feelings and share them with the group. It also helps us stay grounded in the present moment.

In this process, we are encouraged to stay in the present moment and asked not to bring up the past, unless we are experiencing feelings right now that are connected to past events. If the feelings are coming up now, then they are part of our present experience. If not, then we are "reaching" for something to share about, rather than waiting until something comes up for us that we really want to share.

We all have very complicated stories and sometimes have a tendency to want to convey every detail of our lives to the group when we have its attention. This is not appropriate. The group doesn't need to know our life history. It just invites us to talk about what is happening for us right now. If nothing is happening, we are encouraged to remain in a listening mode.

We should share when we feel moved to speak, much as people share at Quaker meetings. When our heart starts beating and words arise spontaneously in our minds, we can be sure that the Spirit within is prompting us to speak. Often we don't know what words to use but, if we just start speaking, the words come. The Spirit within us knows what we need to communicate. When we can be patient and trusting of our own process, it will be clear when it's time to speak up.

In sharing, we are encouraged to be as honest with ourselves as we can be. We are not in the group to gain support at the expense of any other human being. Often, we may have something coming up about someone at home who is not present in the group. When we speak about this, our focus should not be on the other person, but on ourselves. We are encouraged not to blame or shame anyone in the group or outside it, but to focus on our own thoughts, feelings and experiences and to take responsibility for them.

3. *When our Judgments come up about someone, we will be aware of them and gently bring our attention back to the person speaking.*

One of the immediate revelations we have when we begin working with the Affinity Process is just how many judgments we have about other people. When this happens, we have a tendency to beat ourselves up for having judgments. We tell ourselves "Look at yourself. You aren't a very spiritual person. You have so many judgments." In other words, we judge the judgment. And then we judge the judgment of the judgment.

If we don't catch this downward spiral of judgment

somewhere, it will continue indefinitely. The way we catch it is to accept the fact that we are making judgments. We just witness the phenomenon. We become aware that we are judging. And we hold this awareness gently. We don't beat ourselves up. We don't call ourselves names. We just become aware of our judgments.

Then, we own the judgments. We remember: "every judgment I have is about me, not about the other person. There is some part of me that does not feel acceptable or loved." We allow our awareness to show us that wounded part of ourselves if it can do so. But we stay in our hearts. We don't intellectualize the awareness. We don't go up into our heads.

Then, very gently, we realize that we have been distracted away from the person sharing. We haven't been listening to him or her. We haven't been holding a safe space. We've been judging. We've been finding fault. So we let our awareness sink back into our hearts. And we start to listen again. We hear what the person is saying. We become emotionally present for the person who is speaking.

This process happens every time we become aware that we have been judging. So we get plenty of practice being compassionate with ourselves.

While our goal is to create a safe, non-judgmental space for others in the group, the truth is that we are not always feeling safe ourselves. And when we don't feel safe, it's hard to create safety for others.

When we own our judgments, we get in touch with our own discomfort, instead of blaming others for it. Then, we can be more honest about our own experience.

It seems that we are judging others. But the truth is that we are judging ourselves. If we don't project, but instead get in touch with our judgment of self, we can share with the group more authentically. We can say: "I'm really finding fault with myself right now." And that honesty will bring the group right into its authentic process.

The great irony of the Affinity Process is that our ability to create a safe, loving space enables our judgments to come up into our conscious awareness more readily. To the extent that we feel safe in the group, we can become aware of our judgments without beating ourselves up for having them. When we do that, our judgments may dissolve and we may be able to bring our attention back to the person speaking. But, if our judgments persist, honesty may prompt us to own them not just to ourselves, but to the group. Our willingness to take responsibility for our judgments and bring them to the group is testimony not only to our own authenticity, but also to the depth of safety that is present in the group.

4. *We will not interrupt anyone's process. We will give the person sharing our undivided attention. We will not engage in cross-talk.*

One of the cardinal guidelines is that group members never interrupt another person's sharing. If that person is totally out of process and is not following the guidelines, then the facilitator may interrupt that person, but group members may not. Even facilitators are encouraged to find less aggressive ways to confront group members who are out of process. (See Part Three: Manual For Facilitators).

Every person in the group needs to have the opportunity to share and that sharing needs to be respected. Respect for the person's sharing is shown by not interrupting him or her and by not engaging in side conversations with other group members who don't have the floor. We are asked to give the person sharing our total attention.

Furthermore, the measure of our attention is the degree to which we are able to listen to another person's sharing without judging that person or being distracted by our own thoughts. When we listen deeply, we accept the person just the way s/he is. We feel connected to that person in our hearts as we listen to his or her words. We don't need to agree or disagree with what is said. We let our acceptance of what is said be a bridge which connects us to the essence of the other person. This is communion, an experience that cannot be conveyed by words.

5. *We will take thirty seconds in silence to acknowledge each person's sharing.*

When a member is finished sharing, s/he should say "Thank you; I'm finished" or something like this to indicate to the group that s/he is complete. As a further sign of respect for the person who has just shared, we ask that the group hold at least thirty seconds of silence before another person shares. This silence is very important. It discourages people from responding in a reactive way to what has just been shared.

During the silence, people who are feeling triggered should be asking "what does this sharing bring up for me?" They should find a way to take responsibility for whatever thoughts and feelings have come up for them.

Some groups have found that it is helpful to acknowledge each person's sharing by extending their hands and sending loving energy to the person. This is a nice non-verbal way to say: "I have taken your sharing into my heart. I accept it as your truth and I extend my unconditional love to you."

Members who are acknowledged in this way may take time to make eye contact with the other people in the group or, if it feels safer, they may keep their eyes closed and just feel the energy. When they have taken thirty seconds to experience the group's acknowledgment, they simply say "Thank You." This indicates to the rest of the group that the sharing is complete.

6. *We will not monopolize the group's time and attention. We will yield the floor to others in the group who have shared less than we have.*

It is extremely important that we defer to people in the group who have shared less than we have. We must do this even if we think that what we have to say is important. No one in the group should share a second time until every person who has not shared has been offered an opportunity to have the floor.

The length of each sharing is significant. An average sharing is about five minutes. Sharings of ten minutes are not uncommon. If we take more time than this, we may be monopolizing the group's time and attention.

Often, people who are shy will not speak unless there is plenty of silence. The silence gives them permission to share if they really want to. It is often helpful to have ten or fifteen minutes of silence toward the end of a group session if several members have not shared.

Silence provides the opportunity for some of the more reticent members of the group to share. However, sharing is voluntary. It is not necessary for all members to share in every group session. However, it is essential that each person have "the opportunity" to share.

7. *We will make "I" Statements, not "You" statements. We will take responsibility for our own experiences and respect the experience of others. We will not assign "our" meaning to something someone else has said.*

One of the key awarenesses of the Affinity Process is that everything that we think, feel or experience belongs to us, not to anyone else. If this is true, and we maintain that it is, then it should not be necessary for us to talk about anyone else. Someone in the group or outside of the group may be triggering us, but how we are thinking or feeling is our responsibility. We can take responsibility best when we make "I" statements, when we tell what we are thinking and feeling, and avoid making "You" statements or "S/he" statements.

When members take responsibility for what they are thinking and feeling in the moment, it is easier to stay present with their sharing. We can feel that they are being genuine. We can listen with our hearts as well as our ears.

On the other hand, when members need to talk about other people and have difficulty owning their own thoughts and feelings, it is harder for us to stay present for them. Yet, this is good practice for us. If we find ourselves making the judgment that "Peter is not in the process . . . he's not owning his stuff . . . he's not taking responsibility," we get to see that our buttons are being pushed. Perhaps we are projecting our own issues onto Peter. Maybe we don't stay in the process either. While on the surface we are judging Peter, underneath we are really judging ourselves. That's an important realization. So we make note of that and then bring our attention back to Peter. He is an equal brother, after all. He's having the same difficulty we have. Now, instead of judging him, we can listen to him with compassion.

It is always good practice for us to own our judgments as they come up. Owning our judgments immediately restores our sense of equality with the person sharing and enables us to be authentically present with him or her.

Having had all these judgments about Peter, I might decide to share with the group what my experience just was. After the thirty seconds of silence, I might say to the group. "I'd just like to acknowledge that my buttons are being pushed tonight. I have been making judgments about how people are sharing and thinking that they are not in the process. I've been looking at my judgments, and realizing that I'm projecting, that in fact I haven't been in the process. I haven't really been authentic in my sharing. Here I am judging you guys when I'm really feeling inadequate myself. I'm realizing just how hard it is for me to really tell the truth about what is going on for me. It's hard for me to trust you with what I'm really thinking and feeling because that means I will be vulnerable, and I'm not sure I want to be vulnerable. It's easier for me to hold back and make judgments about you than to look at myself."

This communication is honest and it takes total responsibility for my experience. I don't put Peter on the spot, because he is just the trigger. My comments are about me, not about Peter or about others in the group.

Of course, I could have said "Peter, your sharing brought up a lot of stuff for me. I was really judging you, but I know that's a projection. It's really about me, not you." That is still good process, but why single Peter out unless he repeatedly triggers me? Whenever we single out another person, we run the risk that we are blaming and shaming. Or even if we aren't, the other person may take it that way.

When we find that one person pushes our buttons over and over again, we might want to ask that person to meet with us for some Affinity sharing after the group ends. Often, it is more sensitive and effective to communicate these issues one to one than it is in front of the group. However, when we do this, it is very important to stay in the Affinity Process so that each person gets to speak and own his or her thoughts and feelings without being interrupted.

8. *We will not hide our hurt or angry feelings. We will share them honestly, without trying to make others responsible for how we feel.*

When we share, we are trusting the group to respect our sharing and to hold it gently and lovingly. We hope that others will deal with any judgments they have about us and own them. But sometimes group members may go way out of process and verbalize a judgment about something that we said. Or they may interpret something we said according to their own life experience or conceptual filters.

For example, suppose after Peter finished speaking, I shared this: "I'm feeling that some people in the group are sharing superficially and are not being honest about their experience." That is clearly a judgment that I'm making and I'm not owning it in any way. Even though I don't mention Peter, Peter assumes that by the words "some people" I mean him, since he just finished sharing.

Peter doesn't say anything back, but he refuses to look at me for the rest of the group session. When he leaves, he hugs everyone in the group except me. Obviously, Peter is feeling judged and attacked by me. Unless he realizes this and owns it, he will continue to act toward me in passive/aggressive ways. The energy between us will be difficult. It will be hard for us to be in the group together.

This guideline would encourage Peter to speak up about how he feels. Ideally, he would do this right after I verbalized my judgment. If not then, he might do it later in the group or at the beginning of the next meeting. For example, he might say: "I'd like to share first today. Last week, I felt that my sharing was discounted when you (Paul) said you felt that 'some people' were not sharing authentically. I felt hurt by what you said, even though I realized that you were probably right. It is hard for me to tell the truth about how I'm feeling. I'm afraid if I do you will reject me. Well, I felt rejected anyway. So it really pushed my buttons. I didn't even want to come to the group today. My pattern is to run away when I feel that others don't accept me. But I realized that I had to come tonight and tell the truth about how I was feeling, even if it meant that I would get rejected again. 'Cause I know that my pattern is not to hang in there, not to stand up for myself, not to give others the chance to know me. I've been thinking about this all week. And I'm glad I had the guts to come here and say this. It feels like a real breakthrough for me."

Peter is touching reality deeply. He is owning his feelings, being authentic, and letting me know what my judgment brought up for him without blaming me. That helps me to see the effect of my own behavior. It helps me to see that I have many of the same issues that Peter has. Perhaps that is why I tend to find fault with him. He is a good mirror for me. And now he is modeling the process for me in a way that I can really learn from. His courageous honesty is making it possible for me to be honest with myself and others. He is showing me how to tell the truth and take responsibility at the same time.

9. *If someone shares a hurt or angry feeling with us, we will acknowledge how s/he feels. We will not defend ourselves or try to justify our words or actions. We will share any feelings that come up for us.*

Let's take a different scenario in the above situation. Let's say Peter decided to tell the truth about how he was feeling right after I made my judgment of him. Suppose he said: "I need to share again. I'm feeling very hurt and angry about what you just shared, Paul. It seems to me that you were making a judgment about my sharing when you said 'some people are sharing superficially.' I'm not feeling very safe or honored being in this group right now."

This communication is clear, authentic, and responsible. It helps me to see how my actions have affected someone else. This guideline asks me to take this information in without defending myself. I just need to acknowledge what Peter is saying, not to agree with him or to take responsibility for how he feels. I am not responsible for how Peter feels, even if I triggered him. My focus must always be on me, not on Peter. If Peter's sharing brought up feelings for me, then I need to take time to get in touch with those feelings and share them with the group when I'm ready.

10. *We will stay in the present moment. We will not bring up the past or future, unless they are happening for us here and now.*

This process is most effective when we deal with what we are thinking and feeling right now. The present is the place of power and creativity.

To stay in the present, we must trust the silence. When we first ask ourselves if there is anything which is heavy on our hearts, anything that is causing us to feel anxious, afraid, guilty, judgmental toward ourselves or others, we may not be aware of anything. If that's the case, we should remain silent until something surfaces in our awareness that we know we should share.

As participants we are discouraged from giving a book report on our activities during the last week. Even if something upsetting happened to us during the week, we would share that only if it still felt unresolved.

On the other hand, even when we think that nothing is up for us, we can be unexpectedly triggered by someone else's sharing. When we find ourselves strongly agreeing/disagreeing with, or making judgments about, something someone else has said, we know that our own issues are coming up for healing. Sharing at such a time can be authentic, if we have the courage to tell the truth about what we're thinking and feeling without blaming the person who triggered us.

11. *We will keep everything that is said in the group confidential.*

Since group members will often share intimate details of their lives in the Affinity Group, it is essential that everyone in the group keep what is shared confidential. This means that the information does not leave the group.

Just as you don't want another member telling details about your private life to a spouse or a friend, you need to refrain from sharing private information you have about other members of the group. This is an opportunity for you to practice the golden rule: "Do unto others as you would have them do unto you."

You are advised not to talk with any member of the group about some other member's sharing. That is a violation of the agreement to keep everyone's sharing confidential. Such violations compromise the safety and trust in a group like nothing else.

In order for the group to continue to feel safe, members need to be comfortable sharing from their hearts. Confidentiality builds continued trust and safety. Remember, you demonstrate your unconditional love and acceptance of other group members not only during the group, but when you go home as well.

12. ***We will honor the silence, knowing that it offers us an opportunity to become more deeply present to ourselves and others.***

The silence is the healing agent in the Affinity Group. Spirit always works in the silence, helping us to move into our hearts and connect more deeply with ourselves and others. It is in the silence that we learn to hold our judgments with compassion. It is in the silence that we own our own fear, instead of projecting it onto another group member.

Our awareness works in the silence. Just by being aware of our fears and judgments without beating ourselves up we begin to rest in a deeper and more peaceful state of consciousness. This is the existential ground of our being, the place of simple awareness in which the breath comes and goes and the events and circumstances of our lives are accepted as they are. In this state, we do not struggle with our lives. We do not judge ourselves or others. When we rest in this place, we know that everything that is happening is perfect just the way it is.

Silence takes us into this place. That is why we mustn't be afraid when people in the group stop talking. It is indeed a great blessing. By staying with the silence, those who really need to speak will be given permission. The group consciousness will deepen until the feeling of love is almost palpable.

If you have ever been to a Quaker meeting in which the silence is held deeply, you know the power of the presence that manifests when people practice unconditional love and acceptance of one another. That presence is so deeply healing and all-embracing that words are not necessary. Indeed, words often break the energy and bring people out of their hearts.

I always tell people that when you sit in the silence, you won't have any doubt about when it's time to share. Your heart will start beating, your hands will start sweating, your chair will start shaking and you will feel called to speak without knowing what is going to come out of your mouth.

When this happens, you aren't speaking from your ego or limited consciousness. You are speaking from your heart and opening to whatever healing you need at the time.

While the goal of the Affinity Group Process is not to heal anyone, healing does happen. It is a by-product of acceptance and compassion. It is one of the paradoxes of spiritual life that healing comes not when we seek it, but when we open our hearts wide enough to give and receive unconditional love. For only love heals. No technique or process in and of itself can heal.

When we surrender into the silence, we come fully into the present moment. We sink down through our fears and our judgments. We breathe and accept. We open our hearts. We make peace within and without. We become host to the presence of the love, whose greatest joy is to abide in our hearts.

13. *If we feel that the group is going "off-purpose," we will ask for a moment of silence, during which our group can re-center and remember its purpose.*

It is easy to judge others and react to their behavior. The Affinity Group Guidelines help us to be aware of our judgments so that we don't react to other people in the group. But we don't always practice the guidelines. We make mistakes.

It doesn't help the group to single someone out and say "You aren't following the guidelines." Even if this statement is true, it can be experienced as an attack. Whenever anyone in the group is criticized or attacked, it makes the space feel less safe for everyone. To avoid making others wrong, we simply ask for a moment of silence when we are not feeling safe in the group. We request this silence in between sharings. We don't interrupt anyone's process to ask for a moment of silence.

Any request for silence should be honored by the group unless someone already has the floor. During the silence, members try to re-center, observe their thoughts and feelings, and remember that the purpose of the group is to provide a loving space where it is safe to share.

It is amazing to see how effective such moments of silence are in helping to return the group to its purpose.

Silence helps us breathe, center, accept and deepen in our experience. I am always amazed by its power to bring us back to love and acceptance.

14. *Remembering that we won't do this process perfectly, we will be gentle with ourselves and use whatever transpires in the group as an opportunity to practice forgiveness.*

The Affinity Group is a slice of life. It is never perfect. We make mistakes. We don't follow the guidelines, even though we clearly intend to. Both facilitators and members say inappropriate things. We don't always stay in our hearts. We aren't always present for those who are sharing.

Often, we push each other's buttons and feel hurt or angry. We slip into blaming or shaming. We blow it.

That's not the end of things. In some ways, it is really the beginning. When we feel safe enough in our group to totally lose it, we are sharing ourselves on a whole different level. Then, we experience what it is like to be held compassionately when we think we least deserve the love and acceptance of others. To receive that kind of unconditional love, as well as to offer it to others, can be profoundly healing.

No matter how far the group strays from its purpose, it can always return to it. Any mistake can be acknowledged and learned from. Every time we go "out of process" we have an opportunity to see our detour and recommit to the process. We don't have to beat ourselves up. We don't have to feel guilty for making a mistake. We just need to say: "I guess we're all being hard on ourselves here. Let's take some time in silence to be in forgiveness of what just happened and to remember why we are here."

Without the practice of forgiveness, we cannot experience genuine intimacy with others. The more the group bonds, the more even subtle violations of the process stand out and beg for correction. When we can acknowledge and forgive our mistakes on an ongoing basis, we can continue our journey into greater and greater intimacy.

Commentary on Group Agreements

1. *We agree to honor the purpose of the group.*

The purpose of the group is to give and receive unconditional love, acceptance and support, to create a safe, loving, non-judgmental space in which we can open our hearts and move through our fears. If we are going to participate in the Affinity Process, we must be aligned with this purpose and willing to remember it constantly as our reason for coming together as a group.

2. *We agree to practice the guidelines.*

The Affinity Group guidelines are the vehicle through which the purpose of the group is achieved. The purpose tells us what we wish to accomplish together. The guidelines tell us how we are going to accomplish our goal.

When joining a group, it is essential that each member

understands and accepts the guidelines. People who don't feel comfortable with the purpose statement or the guidelines should not join an Affinity Group.

Members' willingness to be guided by the purpose statement and to follow the guidelines is the agreement that binds them together. It is important that this agreement be emphasized on an ongoing basis. To accomplish this, members are asked to read the purpose statement and the guidelines aloud at the beginning of every meeting.

3. *We agree to be on time for every group meeting.*

Many groups have found it demoralizing when some of its members are late to meetings. When members are late, the group has to wait until they arrive so that their entrance will not be disruptive to the group process.

To avoid potential problems, it is suggested that each member of the group be responsible for arriving at least ten or fifteen minutes early so that the group can begin and end on time. This respects the time commitment made by other members, some of whom may need to leave punctually to be home for children or other commitments.

4. *We agree to attend every meeting of the group.*

When joining an Affinity Group, members need to realize that they are making an 8–10 week commitment. This commitment is important because it facilitates group bonding and ensures a continuity of experience for members of the group.

Participants should join the group with the intention of coming to every meeting. When emergencies come up that must be dealt with, the group member involved is asked to let the facilitator know that s/he won't be able to attend that meeting.

The stability of the group membership helps to maintain the feeling of safety and trust in the group. Each member contributes to that stability by making a point to be on time and attend every session of the group.

Facilitating a Group

Ideally, individuals would participate in an Affinity Group for eight to ten weeks before attempting to facilitate a group. This gives them invaluable experience with the process and, with it, the understanding and self-confidence required to facilitate a group on their own.

Prospective facilitators are also encouraged to attend the Affinity Retreats which I try to hold at least once each year. These retreats bring together Affinity Group facilitators and participants from all over the world.

Clearly, the more experience you have with the Affinity Process, the easier it will be for you to facilitate a group. But it may be that there aren't any Affinity Groups happening in your area and it's up to you to be the pioneer in starting a group. If that's the case, don't despair. Our website (www.paulferrini.com) has the names of experienced facilitators you can contact for some coaching as you prepare to facilitate your first group.

Part Three: Practice

A MANUAL FOR FACILITATORS

Putting a Group Together

If you wish to start an Affinity Group, invite friends and interested people* to a guest evening during which the Process can be introduced. Share with the group why you are attracted to the Affinity Group Process and how you feel it might help you. Review the purpose statement and the guidelines and ask if there are any questions. If possible, have copies of this book on hand that people can buy and take home and read.

If you are offering to facilitate the group in your home, suggest two or three times when it would be convenient for you to host the group. Remember, it is rare that all interested people will agree on a single time, so pass around a sheet of paper with the alternative meeting times highlighted and have people put their names down under the times they can commit to. If there are enough people interested to make two groups, ask if there is anyone else who would be willing to facilitate and host a group in their home.

In some cases, you may need to have more than one guest evening before pinning down the logistics of group meetings. It is better to take a little more time in the beginning to be sure that group members are committed to the proposed meeting times than to find out later that people have dropped out of the group because

* If you need help finding interested people, we can provide you with names and addresses of people in your area who have purchased books and/or participated in programs we have done in the past.

of scheduling conflicts. Try as much as you can to make sure that everyone in your group is committed to the eight to ten week process before you have the first Affinity Group session.

As mentioned previously, the ideal group size is eight to twelve members. If you have more than twelve people, there may not be sufficient time for everyone to share during the two hour session. Groups with less than eight people will often have less diversity and may invite overly long sharings from members. In the prototype group of eight to twelve members, each member is sharing about 10% of the time and listening 90% of the time. As you can see, the speaking/listening balance is heavily weighted toward listening in the Affinity Process. This ensures that members learn to be present for others and also learn to listen more deeply to their own inner dialog.

This being said, it must be acknowledged that the Affinity Process can be practiced wherever "two or more gather together." When the situation necessitates, smaller groups are acceptable. Larger groups can also work if participants are skilled in the Process. I have facilitated groups as large as one hundred people using the Affinity Process. However, these larger groups work because participants have had previous experience in smaller groups.

The more diverse group membership is the better. Groups that incorporate people of different gender, age group, religious, cultural or racial heritage are ideal, since the Affinity Group strives not for agreement, but for acceptance and respect for each person's experience.

Service and Spiritual Practice

The Affinity Group provides people with a spiritual practice that can uplift their lives. I don't believe that there should be a price associated with spiritual practice. I believe it should be available to all who want it and are willing to commit to it. Members who are in a position to contribute financially and wish to support the Affinity Group Process worldwide can made a tax deductible contribution or tithe to *The Miracles Community Network*.

Group members are asked to express their gratitude for the gift of the Process by extending it to others. By helping other people learn these important skills, each member can have an exponential impact on the lives of others. This is the way the process extends. It is an organic ministry spreading the teaching and practice of unconditional love, acceptance, and forgiveness.

While trainings and support services to facilitators may sometimes involve a fee, weekly Affinity Group meetings need to be free of charge. The only exception would be if a public space needed to be rented to house the group. In that case, a love offering could be taken from members to help pay for the rental expense.

Opening a Meeting

The following guidelines will help you facilitate the opening of your Affinity Group meeting:

1. *Wait until everyone arrives before beginning the meeting.*

2. *Gather people in a circle and hold hands. Then say "I want to remind all of us that we're here to create a safe, loving, non-judgmental space where we can open our hearts and move through our fears. Let's take a few moments now in silence to become emotionally present, connect with each other in our hearts and remember why we have gathered together." After a few moments of silence, you can ask the group to sit down and then ask members to take turns reading the guidelines aloud. After that, you can declare the floor open for sharing.*

Closing a Meeting

When the group is about twenty minutes away from its agreed-on ending time, wait for a pause in the sharing and say: "I just want to remind the group that we have only ten or fifteen minutes left for sharing before we go into our closing. I want to ask those of us who have already shared to hold the space for those who have not shared yet. And I want to ask those who have not shared to check inside and see if there's anything you'd like to share at this time. Please don't take this a pressure to speak, but as an opportunity to share if you are ready."

If silence persists, check in with the group one more time: "I just want to let everyone know that we have four or five minutes left: time for one person to share who hasn't shared yet." When the time is up, tell the group "Okay, it is time for us to go into our closing."

Always leave at least five minutes for the closing ritual. Again, gather the group in a circle and hold hands. Ask the group members to close their eyes and say "I want to thank all of you for speaking and listening from your hearts today. We hold what has been communicated with compassion and confidentiality. We are grateful for everyone's contribution. Thank you all for the gift you bring to this group." Then close with a Sufi Song and Dance such as *May the Blessings of God Rest Upon You* or *All I ask of you is forever to remember me as loving you.**

When to Intervene

It is suggested that the facilitator intervene only when someone in the group is way out of process. Examples include: cross talk (a sample intervention would be "Excuse me, but I'd like to ask us all to give the speaker our full attention. Thank You."), overt judgment

---

*The cassette tape "The Songs of Joy" contains many songs and dances we do in our meetings, conferences, and retreats. A copy of the tape is $10 and can be ordered through Heartways Press.

of or feedback about what someone else has shared (a sample intervention would be "I wonder if we could all remember to make I statements, not you statements. It's most helpful if we talk about ourselves, not others. Thanks.") interrupting a person's sharing (a sample intervention would be "Bob, could I ask you to wait until Susan is finished sharing? Thank you."), and monopolizing the group's time and attention (a sample intervention would be "Excuse me, Walter. I'm very sorry to interrupt you. I wonder if you would be willing to complete your sharing in the next few minutes, so that we make sure that everyone has a chance to share? Thank you for understanding").

The need for such interventions will be minimal when group members take the time to understand the guidelines. If you find that you are having to intervene a lot, you might want to take five or ten minutes at the beginning of the next group to clarify a couple of the guidelines you feel people aren't understanding. Try to do this in a general way, without using any of the group members as examples. That way, no one feels judged or picked on.

If you are a new facilitator without Affinity Group experience be honest with the group from the start. Say something like: "I want everyone to know that I'm a novice at this process, just like you. I'm willing to play the role of facilitator, but I'd like to ask all of you to help me. Let me know after the group if you didn't feel supported and safe at any point in the process. I'm sure there will be times when I intervene inappropriately or don't intervene when I should. Please understand that I'm probably going to make some mistakes. If you are ever really uncomfortable with anything that happens in the group, ask for a moment of silence, so that we can get back on track. That way each one of you will be helping me."

Even if you are an experienced facilitator, some version of the above disclaimer statement should be made. The strongest Affinity Groups are the ones in which every member takes responsibility for following the guidelines. In such groups, a facilitator is not really necessary. Or to put it another way, in such groups, everyone facilitates.

If you make your role as facilitator too important, you will put a lot of pressure on yourself and get in the way of members taking their share of responsibility for the success of the process. Your best move as facilitator is to model the process by being authentic and responsible in your own sharings. This will empower the other group members to do the same.

How to Intervene

When possible, do not interrupt someone's sharing. Remind the group about following an important guideline during a pause in the sharing. Also try not to put any group member on the spot. Make general comments using the word "we" instead of "you."

For example, suppose that a sharing lasts fifteen minutes and focuses primarily on a past event with lots of "story" details. When that sharing concludes and is completely received by the group, you might say "I want to remind us that it's important to stay in the present and to communicate what we are thinking and feeling right now. Does anyone have anything that is coming up right now that s/he would like to share?" Interventions like this help to shift the energy back to authentic process and away from storytelling.

The most important thing you should ask yourself as a facilitator before you make any intervention is "Can I say this in a loving way?" If the person sharing is pushing your buttons and you find yourself getting angry or impatient, then you know you can't intervene in a loving way. At such times, you must become aware of what's happening in your own consciousness and take responsibility for that before you can begin to facilitate.

In this case, you also have a real opportunity to model the process by acknowledging your own fears and judgments. For example, you might say "I want to own that I have a lot of judgments coming up right now. I'm being triggered by some of the sharing. I'm wondering if we are following the process here and I want to intervene as a facilitator, but I know that if I do I won't be coming from love. I'll be coming from frustration. I feel frustrated. I don't think we're doing it right and I think it's my responsibility to fix it. And I know we're not here to fix each other. But I want to fix all of you. And I guess that means I'm not doing it right either. I guess I think that if we don't do it right, it's my fault. I'm to blame. . . . Yeah, that's it. I just wanted to own that. Thank you."

This communication helps the group stay in the present because you are sharing a present reality. It encourages other people to do the same.

As a rule of thumb, don't intervene as a facilitator if you can't do so in a loving way. If you are being triggered, the person who is triggering you will know it even if you say all the right "facilitator" words. If you have judgments or feelings coming up, you need to let go of your facilitator hat, and tell the group what is up for you. By participating authentically in the process, you model it for others.

Facilitator Styles

There are two extremes in facilitating a group. One extreme is to be what we call "a gestapo for the guidelines." A gestapo for the guidelines is constantly intervening to try to get people on track in the group. When there is too much intervention in a group, people don't feel safe sharing. They become afraid that the facilitator will interrupt them or criticize their sharing and they start to withhold.

The other facilitation extreme is to let everyone share with minimal intervention. When cross talk, monopolizing, interrupting, and verbal judgments are happening in the group, people don't feel safe sharing their thoughts and feelings with other group members. In this case, the facilitator is not adequately standing up for the guidelines.

Obviously both of these extremes are to be avoided.

The best facilitators let the small things go and confront only the most obvious violations of the guidelines. When they do confront, they try to do so in a loving, supportive way. They try not to put any member on the spot.

A good facilitator may also use the time before or after the group to share concerns with individual members who might be out of process. Often, it is easier to give feedback on a one to one basis than it is in front of the whole group. And it's also easier to check in with that person to see how s/he feels about the feedback.

Clear but harmonious facilitation is an art. You have to constantly keep checking in with yourself to make sure that you are coming from a positive, helpful place. You have to be continually sensitive to the other members of the group to make sure they feel accepted and honored. And you have to be honest when you are being triggered so that people can hold the space for you too.

The more experience you have with the Affinity Process, the more your facilitation skills will deepen. If you have a co-facilitator, you can help each other understand when an intervention backfires and decreases safety in the group and when an intervention would have been appropriate and helpful to the group. If you have an Affinity Coordinator in your area, you can hone your facilitation skills by participating in support groups for facilitators. And you can also deepen your skills by attending the yearly Christ Mind/Affinities Retreat where you will be able to share the Affinity experience with other facilitators from around the world.

Evaluation and Extension

One way members can track their growth from week to week through the process is to keep an Affinity Journal. Questionnaire 1 in the Appendix provides a list of questions which can be used as a springboard for journaling. When journal entries are reviewed after the eight week process is over, participants gain a real concrete sense of what they have learned during the Affinity Group.

Questionnaire 2 in the Appendix is yet another evaluation tool. It should be passed out to all members during the eighth meeting. They can then fill it out and bring it to the final group session, during which members will be asked to share what they have learned during the group and to consider how they plan to continue working with the process in the future.

It should be pointed out that, although the Process itself takes eight weeks, the total commitment for members is ten weeks. The ten weeks includes an orientation session (or guest evening) at the beginning and an evaluation session at the end.

During the evaluation session, take about a forty-five minutes to an hour to invite members to share (using the affinity guidelines) about their experience in the group, what they have learned, how they have grown, and how their practice of the Affinity Group guidelines has made an impact in their daily lives. Then remind members that they have completed part one of the Affinity Group Process. Part two happens when they make a specific commitment to extend the process in some other area of their lives. Take another twenty or thirty minutes and invite members to share how they might offer the Affinity Process to other people who could benefit from it.

You might begin by telling the group what you plan to do. Perhaps you will be starting another Affinity Group or maybe you will be offering a support group for facilitators. If you plan to offer a support group, be sure to give the details and invite all members of your group to attend it. Tell them that attending the group is very important if they plan to facilitate or co-facilitate an Affinity Group.

If members don't feel ready to facilitate or co-facilitate, you can invite them to join another Affinity Group. That group will have different members from the current group. It may be facilitated by you or by someone else in the group. Before you end the Affinity portion of the meeting, make sure members know how and when you will be following up with them about future Affinity Groups.

Some groups may wish to take a break of a month or so before beginning another Affinity Group cycle. During this time, guest evenings can be offered for new participants and new groups can be put together.

End the meeting with a pot luck dinner or snack and plenty of time for people to socialize. It's good to allow about three hours for this last session of the group. The first two hours can be devoted to Affinity Group concerns and the last hour can be devoted to eating and socializing.

Building An Affinity Community

When several members of your Affinity Group decide to extend the process somewhere in the community and commit to attend a support group for facilitators once or twice a month, the Affinity Community begins to take shape. Ideally, each facilitator who concludes a group would move into a facilitator support role, and each member of the group would become a facilitator. If we take the prototype group of eight members plus the facilitator, this progression would result in eight new Affinity Groups, plus a support group for facilitators.

As a participant, you move from belonging to a small group of eight to twelve people to playing a leadership role in a community of seventy or eighty people. You stay involved in the process so that you can continue your spiritual practice, and you experience the joy of helping a whole new group of people learn these important skills.

As the Affinity community grows, it may be helpful to have periodic gatherings that bring all the groups together. A typical gathering might be held on a Sunday. In the morning, there could be an interfaith worship service, a major part of which would involve creating an Affinity Space or sacred silence, from which participants could share whatever is coming up for them. The service could also include some devotional singing, sufi dancing, and/or other activities that help people connect emotionally with each other. An afternoon program might involve a pot luck picnic lunch and other fun social activities that would appeal both to group members and their friends and families.*

At this stage of the development, the community may wish to consider electing an Affinity Coordinator. A tithing program can be instituted at this time to provide financial support for the Coordinator.

Those persons who feel committed to the Affinity Group Process and to the Affinity Community should consider making a pledge of $10 per week (or more if they can afford it) to support the Coordinator and cover his or her expenses.

If you are considering working toward becoming an Affinity Coordinator, you must realize that it may take a year or two before any financial support will be possible from the local Affinity Community. Only your love for the process, your commitment to it, and your willingness to offer your time and energy as service will guide you through this initial phase of building the Affinity Community. Your dedication will be obvious to the people you serve. And they, in turn, will want to do what they can to provide for you.

The Miracles Community Network, the international educational organization supporting Affinity Groups worldwide, seeks to support coordinators and their member Affinity Groups through trainings and retreats.

If these occasional Affinity gatherings are popular, they can be offered more frequently, perhaps on a monthly basis. Eventually, the Affinity Community may expand sufficiently to support weekly gatherings that include an Interfaith worship service.

As funds are raised, the Network might also be able to offer support through a newsletter, a web site, and other related services.

Appendix

GROUP EVALUATION QUESTIONNAIRES

Questionnaire 1

WEEKLY AFFINITY JOURNAL ENTRY

Use the following questions as a springboard for writing about your experience in your Affinities Journal. As a result of your journaling, you may find that there are some issues coming up for you that you want to share with the group.

1. What were the most difficult moments for you during this group? What pushed your buttons? When did your fears and/or judgments come up?

2. Were you able to hold your fears and judgments in a compassionate way or did you beat yourself up?

3. To what extent do you feel that you were really able to be present for other people's sharings?

4. Do you feel that you were able to be really honest in your sharing in the group today?

5. Do you feel that your sharing was honored by the other people in the group?

6. Did your sharing and the group's holding of it result in any kind of shift in your perception of your situation? If so, what is the nature of that shift?

7. Is there a particular person in this group onto whom you tend to project your issues? Please elaborate.

8. Did the group feel safe to you today?

9. Was there a time when you felt the group really got off track and strayed from the guidelines? How might this have been avoided?

10. Are you understanding this process better? If so, how? Which aspects of this process would you like clarified? Can you bring these questions up to the group at the beginning of the next meeting?

Questionnaire 2

AFFINITY GROUP EVALUATION

Your answers to these questions will prepare you for the final session of the Affinity Group. Please take time to consider each question and answer it as completely as you can. If you kept an Affinities Journal, take time to read through it before you answer these questions.

PART 1: EVALUATION OF THIS AFFINITY GROUP

1. What did you learn most from this Affinity Group? About Yourself? About Others?

2. Did you feel safe in the group and were you able to tell the truth about your experience? How did this change over the eight weeks?

3. Do you feel that you were able to be present for other people's sharings in your group? How did this change over time?

4. Does listening to others without judgment and sharing honestly with others mean something different to you now than they did when you started this group? What is different in your understanding?

5. What was the most challenging aspect of this group for you and how did you deal with it?

6. How have you been able to apply the Affinity Group guidelines in your daily life?

PART 2: EXTENDING THE AFFINITY PROCESS TO OTHERS.

If this Affinity Group experience has been helpful to you, would you consider extending it to others? You could volunteer to facilitate or co-facilitate a group in your home, at your work, in your children's school, at your church or in some other organization in your community. Often, you can pair up and co-facilitate with another member of your group who is interested in working with a similar population such as teenagers, prisoners, elderly, people with cancer or AIDS, AA members, battered women, homeless people, etc.

To support you, your facilitator may be offering an Affinity Group for Facilitators. Usually a group like this meets once or twice a month and helps to reconnect you with members of your original Affinity Group who, like you, are extending the Process in other areas of the community. Attending such a support group will help you more deeply understand the Affinity Process and facilitate it in your group.

If you don't feel ready to facilitate or co-facilitate a group, you can join another Affinity Group and get another eight weeks of experience under your belt before considering the issue of extending this process to others.

Please use the space below to indicate your future

plans for participating in/facilitating the Affinity Group Process. If, by some chance, you don't wish to continue with the Affinity Process, please use the space below to indicate why.

The Miracles Community Network

Trainings, Facilitator Support Groups, Telephone Support for Facilitators, a Web Site, and a Newsletter linking Affinity Group participants will be developed as funds allow by *The Miracles Community Network,* a non-profit, tax exempt, educational organization devoted to supporting the Affinity Group work worldwide. The Network depends on your financial support to provide these important services. You can get on our mailing list by calling 1-413-774-9474. Tax deductible contributions can be sent to *The Miracles Community Network,* P.O. Box 99, Greenfield, MA. 01302. Please visit our website (www.paulferrini.com) for more information on Affinity Groups in the U.S. and abroad.

Ordering Books for Your Affinity Group

Copies of this book can be ordered from Heartways Press (see order form at the back of this book). If you want to order in bulk, you may be eligible for a discount off the retail cover price.

- 10 or more copies: 10% discount plus shipping
- 20 or more copies: 20% discount plus shipping
- One or more cases: 40% discount plus shipping

Paul Ferrini's unique blend of radical Christianity and other wisdom traditions goes beyond self-help and recovery into the heart of healing. His conferences, retreats, and *Affinity Group Process* have helped thousands of people deepen their practice of forgiveness and open their hearts to the divine presence in themselves and others.

Information on Paul's workshops, retreats or *Affinity Group Process* can be found at ***www.paulferrini.com.*** You can send email to **heartway@crocker.com** or write to **Heartways Press, P. O. Box 99, Greenfield, MA 01302.**

New Releases from Heartways Press

Christ is the light born in the darkness.
He is the rebirth of love in a world driven by fear.

The Living Christ
by Paul Ferrini
ISBN 1-879159-49-X
256 pages paperback $14.95

Paul: Is it true that you are the Christ?

Jesus: Yes, and so are you and everyone else who learns to love and accept self and others. If you practice what I came to teach, you will begin to realize that the Christ nature is the essence of each person. If you see it in me, you must also see it in yourself and in your brother or sister.

Paul: Are you saying the Christ is a sort of collective phenomenon?

Jesus: Yes, Christ is the light born in the darkness. It is the flame of self acceptance that extends to others and eventually to all.

Christ comes at the time of greatest darkness, the time when inner power is ignored and outer power dominates. He is rebirth of love in a world driven by fear.

Opening our Hearts to the Lessons of Love

Dancing with the Beloved
by Paul Ferrini
ISBN 1-879159-47-3
160 pages paperback $12.95

Romance may open the door to love, but it does not help us walk through it. Something else is needed. Something deeper. Something ultimately more real. Challenging times must be weathered. Love must be strengthened beyond neediness and self-interest. It must die a thousand deaths to learn to rise like the phoenix beyond adversity of any kind.

Love is not a fragile, shiny thing, kept separate from the pain and misery of life. It is born of our willingness to learn from our mistakes and encounter the depth of our pain, as well as our partner's pain. That is the way it is.

In time we learn that all pain is the same pain. And we have compassion for the other people who inadvertently step on our toes as they learn to find the inner rhythms of the dance. Like us, they will stumble and fall hundreds of times until that moment of profound acceptance when grace comes and the beloved takes their hand in the circle.

Books and Tapes
available from Heartways Press

Paul Ferrini's luminous new translation captures the essence of Lao Tzu and the fundamental aspects of Taoism in a way that no single book ever has!

The Great Way of All Beings:
Renderings of Lao Tzu
by Paul Ferrini
ISBN 1-879159-46-5
320 pages hardcover $23.00

The Great Way of All Beings: Renderings of Lao Tzu is composed of two different ent versions of Lao Tzu's masterful scripture *Tao Te Ching*. Part one, *River of Light,* is an intuitive, spontaneous rendering of the material that captures the spirit of the *Tao Te Ching,* but does not presume to be a close translation. Part Two is a more conservative translation of the *Tao Te Ching* that attempts as much as possible to stay with the words and images used in the original text. The words and images used in Part One leap out from the center to explore how the wisdom of the Tao touches us today. By contrast, the words and images of Part Two turn inward toward the center, offering a more feminine, receptive version of the material.

"We listen for it, yet its note can't be heard.
We look intently for it, yet its image can't be seen.

Although it has no beginning,
it leads us back to our original nature

Although it has no end,
it helps us come to completion."

A Practical Guide to Realizing your True Nature

*"Enlightenment is the realization of the light that is within
you. It is the conscious recognition and acceptance
of that light. Enlightenment is discovering who
you already are and being it fully."*

Enlightenment for Everyone
by Paul Ferrini
ISBN 1-879159-45-7
160 pages hardcover $16.00

Enlightenment is not contingent on finding the right teacher or having some kind of peak spiritual experience. There's nothing that you need to get, find or acquire to be enlightened. You don't need a priest or rabbi to intercede with God for you. You don't need a special technique or meditation practice. You don't need to memorize scripture or engage in esoteric breathing practices. You simply need to discover who you already are and be it fully. This essential guide to self-realization contains eighteen spiritual practices that will enable you to awaken to the truth of your being. This exquisite hard-cover book will be a life-long companion and will make an inspirational gift to friends and family.

A comprehensive selection from the Christ Mind teachings just released by Doubleday

"Open yourself now to the wisdom of Jesus, as Paul Ferrini has brought it through. These words can inspire you to greater insights and understandings, to more clarity and a grander resolve to make changes in your life that can truly change the world."

Neale Donald Walsch, author of *Conversations with God*.

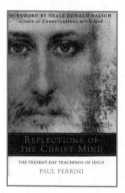

Reflections of the Christ Mind: The Present Day Teachings of Jesus
by Paul Ferrini
Introduction by Neale Donald Walsch
ISBN 0-385-49952-3
302 pages hardcover $19.95

Reflections of the Christ Mind contains key excerpts from *Love Without Conditions, Silence of the Heart, Miracle of Love* and *Return to the Garden*. It presents the most important teachings in the *Christ Mind* series.

I am the Door
by Paul Ferrini
ISBN 1-879159-41-4
288 pages hardcover $21.95

Years ago, Paul Ferrini began hear-ing a persistent inner voice that said "I want you to acknowledge me." He also had a series of dreams in which Jesus appeared to teach him. Later, when Ferrini's relationship with his teacher was firmly established, the four books in the *Reflections of the Christ Mind* series were published. Here, in this lovely lyrical col-lection, we can hear the voice of Jesus speaking directly to us about practical topics of everyday life that are close to our hearts like work and livelihood, relationships, com-munity, forgiveness, spiritual practices, and miracles. When you put this book down, there will no doubt in your mind that the teachings of the master are alive today. Your life will never be the same.

Taking Back Our Schools
by Paul Ferrini
ISBN 1-879159-43-0 $10.95

This book is written for parents who are concerned about the education of their children. It presents a simple idea that could transform the school system in this country. This book does not pretend to have all the answers. It is the start of a conversation. It is chapter one in a larger book that has not yet been written. If you choose to work with these ideas, you may be one of the authors of the chapters to come.

The Way of Peace
by Paul Ferrini
ISBN 1-879159-42-2
256 pages hardcover
$19.95

The Way of Peace is a simple method for connecting with the wisdom and truth that lie within our hearts. The two hundred and sixteen oracular messages in this book were culled from the bestselling *Reflections of the Christ Mind* series by Paul Ferrini.

Open this little book spontaneously to receive inspirational guidance, or ask a formal question and follow the simple divinatory procedure described in the introduction. You will be amazed at the depth and the accuracy of the response you receive.

Like the *I-Ching,* the *Book of Runes,* and other systems of guidance, *The Way of Peace* empowers you to connect with peace within and act in harmony with your true self and the unique circumstances of your life.

Special dice, blessed by the author, are available for using *The Way of Peace* as an oracle. To order, send $3.00 plus shipping.

Grace Unfolding: The Art of Living A Surrendered Life
96 pages paperback $9.95
ISBN 1-879159-37-6

As we surrender to the truth of our being, we learn to relinquish the need to control our lives, figure things out, or predict the future. We begin to let go of our judgments and interpretations and accept life the way it is. When we can be fully present with whatever life brings, we are guided to take the next step on our journey. That is the way that grace unfolds in our lives.

*"The Road to Nowhere is the path through your heart.
It is not a journey of escape.
It is a journey through your pain
to end the pain of separation."*

Illuminations on the Road to
Nowhere
160 pages paperback $12.95
ISBN 1-879159-44-9

There comes a time for all of us when
the outer destinations no longer sat-
isfy and we finally understand that
the love and happiness we seek cannot be found outside of us. It must
be found in our own hearts, on the other side of our
pain.

This book makes it clear that we can no longer rely on
outer teachers or teachings to find our spiritual iden-
tity. Nor can we find who we are in relationships where
boundaries are blurred and one person makes decisions
for another. If we want to be authentic, we can't allow
anyone else to be an authority for us, nor can we allow
ourselves to be an authority for others.

This provocative book challenges many of our basic
assumptions about personal happiness and the meaning of our relationship with others and with God.

The Relationship Book You've Been Waiting For

Creating a Spiritual Relationship: A Guide to Growth and Happiness for Couples on the Path
144 pages paperback $10.95
ISBN 1-879159-39-2

This simple but profound guide to growth and happiness for couples will help you and your partner:

- Make a realistic commitment to each other
- Develop a shared experience that nurtures your relationship
- Give each other the space to grow and express yourselves as individuals
- Communicate by listening without judgment and telling the truth in a non-blaming way
- Understand how you mirror each other
- Stop blaming your partner and take responsibility for your thoughts, feelings and actions
- Practice forgiveness together on an ongoing basis

These seven spiritual principles will help you weather the ups and downs of your relationship so that you and your partner can grow together and deepen the intimacy between you. The book also includes a special section on living alone and preparing to be in relationship and a section on separating with love when a relationship needs to change form or come to completion.

Return to the Garden
Reflections of The Christ Mind,
Part IV
$12.95, Paperback
ISBN 1-879159-35-X

"In the Garden, all our needs were provided for. We knew no struggle or hardship. We were God's beloved. But happiness was not enough for us. We wanted the freedom to live our own lives. To evolve, we had to learn to become love-givers, not just love-receivers.

We all know what happened then. We were cast out of the Garden and for the first time in our lives we felt shame, jealousy, anger, lack. We experienced highs and lows, joy and sorrow. Our lives became difficult. We had to work hard to survive. We had to make mistakes and learn from them.

Initially, we tried to blame others for our mistakes. But that did not make our lives any easier. It just deepened our pain and misery. We had to learn to face our fears, instead of projecting them onto each other.

Returning to the Garden, we are different than we were when we left hellbent on expressing our creativity at any cost. We return humble and sensitive to the needs of all. We return not just as created, but as co-creator, not just as son of man, but also as son of God."

Learn the Spiritual Practice Associated with the Christ Mind Teachings

Living in the Heart The Affinity Process and the Path of Unconditional Love and Acceptance
Paperback $10.95
ISBN 1-879159-36-8

The long awaited, definitive book on the *Affinity Process* is finally here. For years, the *Affinity Process* has been refined by participants so that it could be easily understood and experienced. Now, you can learn how to hold a safe, loving, non-judgmental space for yourself and others which will enable you to open your heart and move through your fears. The *Affinity Process* will help you learn to take responsibility for your fears and judgments so that you won't project them onto others. It will help you learn to listen deeply and without judgment to others. And it will teach you how to tell your truth clearly without blaming others for your experience.

Part One contains an in-depth description of the principles on which the *Affinity Process* is based. Part Two contains a detailed discussion of the *Affinity Group Guidelines*. And Part Three contains a manual for people who wish to facilitate an *Affinity Group* in their community.

If you are a serious student of the *Christ Mind* teachings, this book is essential for you. It will enable you to begin a spiritual practice which will transform your life and the lives of others. It will also offer you a way of extending the teachings of love and forgiveness throughout your community.

Now Finally our Bestselling Title on Audio Tape

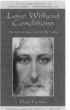

Love Without Conditions,
Reflections of the Christ Mind, Part I
by Paul Ferrini
The Book on Tape Read by the Author
2 Cassettes, Approximately 3.25 hours
ISBN 1-879159-24-4 $19.95

Now on audio tape: the incredible book from Jesus calling us to awaken to our own Christhood. Listen to this gentle, profound book while driving in your car or before going to sleep at night. Elisabeth Kubler-Ross calls this "the most important book I have read. I study it like a Bible." Find out for yourself how this amazing book has helped thousands of people understand the radical teachings of Jesus and begin to integrate these teachings into their lives.

With its heartfelt combination of sensuality and spirituality, Paul Ferrini's poetry has been compared to the poetry of Rumi.

Crossing The Water: Poems About Healing and Forgiveness in Our Relationships

The time for healing and reconciliation has come, Ferrini writes. Our relationships help us heal childhood wounds, walk through our deepest fears, and cross over the water of our emotional pain. Just as the rocks in the river are pounded and caressed to rounded stone, the rough edges of our personalities are worn smooth in the context of a committed relationship. If we can keep our hearts open, we can heal together, experience genuine equality, and discover what it means to give and receive love without conditions.

With its heartfelt combination of sensuality and spirituality, Paul Ferrini's poetry has been compared to the poetry of Rumi. These luminous poems demonstrate why Paul Ferrini is first a poet, a lover and a mystic. Come to this feast of the beloved with an open heart and open ears. 96 pp. paper. ISBN 1-879159-25-2 $9.95.

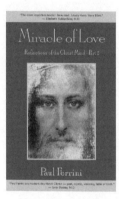

Miracle of Love: Reflections of the Christ Mind, Part III

In this volume of the Christ Mind series, Jesus sets the record straight regarding a number of events in his life. He tells us: "I was born to a simple woman in a barn. She was no more a virgin than your mother was." Moreover, the virgin birth was not the only myth surrounding his life and teaching. So were the concepts of vicarious atonement and physical resurrection.

Relentlessly, the master tears down the rigid dogma and hierarchical teachings that obscure his simple message of love and forgiveness. He encourages us to take him down from the pedestal and the cross and see him as an equal brother who found the way out of suffering by opening his heart totally. We too can open our hearts and find peace and happiness. "The power of love will make miracles in your life as wonderful as any attributed to me," he tells us. "Your birth into this embodiment is no less holy than mine. The love that you extend to others is no less important than the love I extend to you." 192 pp. paper ISBN 1-879159-23-6 $12.95.

The Ecstatic Moment: A Practical Manual for Opening Your Heart and Staying in It.

A simple, power-packed guide that helps us take appropriate responsibility for our experience and establish healthy boundaries with others. Part II contains many helpful exercises and meditations that teach us to stay centered, clear and open in heart and mind. The *Affinity Group Process* and other group practices help us learn important listening and communication skills that can transform our troubled relationships. Once you have read this book, you will keep it in your briefcase or on your bedside table, referring to it often. You will not find a more practical, down to earth guide to contemporary spirituality. You will want to order copies for all your friends. 128 pp. paper ISBN 1-879159-18-X $10.95

The Silence of the Heart: Reflections of the Christ Mind, Part II

A powerful sequel to *Love Without Conditions*. John Bradshaw says: "with deep insight and sparkling clarity, this book demonstrates that the roots of all abuse are to be found in our own self-betrayal. Paul Ferrini leads us skillfully and courageously beyond shame, blame, and attachment to our wounds into the depths of self-forgiveness . . . a must read for all people who are ready to take responsibility for their own healing." 218 pp. paper. ISBN 1-879159-16-3 $14.95

Love Without Conditions: Reflections of the Christ Mind, Part I

An incredible book calling us to awaken to our Christhood. Rarely has any book conveyed the teachings of the master in such a simple but profound manner. This book will help you to bring your understanding from the head to the heart so that you can model the teachings of love and forgiveness in your daily life. 192 pp. paper ISBN 1-879159-15-5 $12.00

The Wisdom of the Self

This ground-breaking book explores our authentic experience and our journey to wholeness. "Your life is your spiritual path. Don't be quick to abandon it for promises of bigger and better experiences. You are getting exactly the experiences you need to grow. If your growth seems too slow or uneventful for you, it is because you have not fully embraced the situations and relationships at hand . . . . To know the Self is to allow everything, to embrace the totality of who we are, all that we think and feel, all of our fear, all of our love." 229 pp. paper ISBN 1-879159-14-7 $12.00

The Twelve Steps of Forgiveness

A practical manual for healing ourselves and our relationships. This book gives us a step-by-step process for moving through our fears, projections, judgments, and guilt so that we can take responsibility for creating the life we want. With great gentleness, we learn to embrace our lessons and to find equality with others. 128 pp. paper ISBN 1-879159-10-4 $10.00

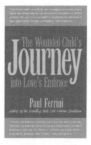

The Wounded Child's Journey: Into Love's Embrace

This book explores a healing process in which we confront our deep-seated guilt and fear, bringing love and forgiveness to the wounded child within. By surrendering our judgments of self and others, we overcome feelings of separation and dismantle co-dependent patterns that restrict our self-expression and ability to give and receive love. 225pp. paper ISBN 1-879159-06-6 $12.00

The Bridge to Reality

A Heart-Centered Approach to *A Course in Miracles* and the Process of Inner Healing. Sharing his experiences of spiritual awakening, Paul emphasizes self-acceptance and forgiveness as cornerstones of spiritual practice. Presented with beautiful photos, this book conveys the essence of The Course as it is lived in daily life. 192 pp. paper ISBN 1-879159-03-1 $12.00

Virtues of The Way

A lyrical work of contemporary scripture reminiscent of the *Tao Te Ching*. Beau-tifully illustrated, this inspirational book will help you cultivate the spiritual values required to fulfill your creative purpose and live in harmony with others. 64 pp. paper ISBN 1-879159-04-X $7.50

From Ego to Self

108 illustrated affirmations designed to offer you a new way of viewing conflict situations so that you can overcome negative thinking and bring more energy, faith and optimism into your life. 144 pp. paper ISBN 1-879159-01-5 $10.00

The Body of Truth

A crystal clear introduction to the universal teachings of love and forgiveness. This book traces all forms of suffering to negative attitudes and false beliefs, which we have the ability to transform. 64 pp. paper   ISBN 1-879159-02-3 $7.50

Available Light

Inspirational, passionate poems dealing with the work of inner integration, love and relationships, death and re-birth, loss and abundance, life purpose and the reality of spiritual vision. 128 pp. paper ISBN 1-879159-05-8 $10.00

Poetry and Guided Meditation Tapes
by Paul Ferrini

The Poetry of the Soul

With its heartfelt combination of sensuality and spirituality, Paul Ferrini's poetry has been compared to the poetry of Rumi. These luminous poems read by the author demonstrate why Paul Ferrini is first a poet, a lover and a mystic. Come to this feast of the beloved with an open heart and open ears. With Suzi Kesler on piano. ISBN 1-879159-26-0 $10.00

The Circle of Healing

The meditation and healing tape that many of you have been seeking. This gentle meditation opens the heart to love's presence and extends that love to all the beings in your experience. A powerful tape with inspirational piano accompaniment by Michael Gray. ISBN 1-879159-08-2 $10.00

Healing the Wounded Child

A potent healing tape that accesses old feelings of pain, fragmentation, self-judgment and separation and brings them into the light of conscious awareness and acceptance. Side two includes a hauntingly beautiful "inner child" reading from The Bridge to Reality with piano accompaniment by Michael Gray. ISBN 1-879159-11-2 $10.00

Forgiveness: Returning to the Original Blessing

A self healing tape that helps us accept and learn from the mistakes we have made in the past. By letting go of our judgments and ending our ego-based search for perfection, we can bring our darkness to the light, dissolving anger, guilt, and shame. Piano accompaniment by Michael Gray. ISBN 1-879159-12-0 $10.00

Paul Ferrini Talks and Workshop Tapes

Answering Our Own Call for Love

Paul tells the story of his own spiritual awakening: his Atheist upbringing, how he began to open to the presence of God, and his connection with Jesus and the Christ Mind teaching. In a very clear, heart-felt way, Paul presents to us the spiritual path of love, acceptance, and forgiveness.
1 Cassette ISBN 1-879159-33-4 $10.00

The Ecstatic Moment

Shows us how we can be with our pain compassionately and learn to nurture the light within ourselves, even when it appears that we are walking through darkness. Discusses subjects such as living in the present, acceptance, not fixing self or others, being with our discomfort and learning that we are lovable as we are. 1 Cassette ISBN 1-879159-27-3 $10.00

Honoring Self and Other

Helps us understand the importance of not betraying ourselves in our relationships with others. Focuses on understanding healthy boundaries, setting limits, and saying no to others in a loving way. Real life examples include a woman who is married to a man who is chronically critical of her, and a gay man who wants to tell his judgmental parents that he has AIDS. 1 Cassette ISBN 1-879159-34-1 $10.00

Seek First the Kingdom

Discusses the words of Jesus in the Sermon on the Mount: "Seek first the kingdom and all else will be added to you." Helps us understand how we create the inner temple by learning to hold our judgments of self and other more compassionately. The love of God flows through our love and acceptance of ourselves. As we establish our connection to the divine within ourselves, we don't need to look outside of ourselves for love and acceptance. Includes fabulous music by The Agape Choir and Band. 1 Cassette   ISBN 1-879159-30-3 $10.00

Double Cassette Tape Sets

Ending the Betrayal of the Self

A roadmap for integrating the opposing voices in our psyche so that we can experience our own wholeness. Delineates what our responsibility is and isn't in our relationships with others, and helps us learn to set clear, firm, but loving boundaries. Our relationships can become areas of sharing and fulfillment, rather than mutual invitations to co-dependency and self betrayal. 2 Cassettes   ISBN 1-879159-28-7 $16.95

Relationships: Changing Past Patterns

Begins with a Christ Mind talk describing the link between learning to love and accept ourselves and learning to love and accept others. Helps us understand how we are invested in the past and continue to replay our old relationship stories. Helps us get clear on what we want and understand how to be faithful to it. By being totally committed to ourselves, we give birth to the beloved within and also without. Includes an in-depth discussion about meditation, awareness, hearing our inner voice, and the Affinity Group Process. 2 Cassettes ISBN 1-879159-32-5 $16.95

Relationship As a Spiritual Path

Explores concrete ways in which we can develop a relationship with ourselves and learn to take responsibility for our own experience, instead of blaming others for our perceived unworthiness. Also discussed: accepting our differences, the new paradigm of relationship, the myth of the perfect partner, telling our truth, compassion vs. rescuing, the unavailable partner, abandonment issues, negotiating needs, when to say no, when to stay and work on a relationship and when to leave. 2 Cassettes ISBN 1-879159-29-5 $16.95

Opening to Christ Consciousness

Begins with a Christ Mind talk giving us a clear picture of how the divine spark dwells within each of us and how we can open up to God-consciousness on a regular basis. Deals with letting go and forgiveness in our relationships with our parents, our children and our partners. A joyful, funny, and scintillating tape you will want to listen to many times. 2 Cassettes ISBN 1-879159-31-7 $16.95

Poster and Notecards

Risen Christ Posters & Notecards
11" x 17"
Poster suitable for framing
ISBN 1-879159-19-8 $10.00

Set of 8
Notecards with Envelopes
ISBN 1-879159-20-1 $10.00

Ecstatic Moment Posters & Notecards

8.5" x 11"
Poster suitable for framing
ISBN 1-879159-21-X $5.00

Set of 8 Notecards with Envelopes
ISBN 1-879159-22-8 $10.00

Heartways Press Order Form

Name _____

Address _____

City _____ State _____ Zip _____

Phone/Fax_____ Email _____

Books by Paul Ferrini

The Living Christ ($14.95)   _____

Dancing with the Beloved ($12.95)   _____

The Great Way of All Beings:
    Renderings of Lao Tzu Hardcover ($23.00) _____

Enlightenment for Everyone Hardcover ($16.00) _____

Taking Back Our Schools ($10.95)   _____

The Way of Peace Hardcover ($19.95)   _____

    Way of Peace Dice ($3.00)   _____

Illuminations on the Road to Nowhere ($12.95) _____

I am the Door Hardcover ($21.95)   _____

Reflections of the Christ Mind Hardcover ($19.95) _____

Creating a Spiritual Relationship ($10.95)   _____

Grace Unfolding: Living a Surrendered Life ($9.95) _____

Return to the Garden ($12.95)   _____

Living in the Heart ($10.95)   _____

Miracle of Love ($12.95)   _____

Crossing the Water ($9.95)   _____

The Ecstatic Moment ($10.95)   _____

The Silence of the Heart ($14.95)   _____

Love Without Conditions ($12.00)   _____

The Wisdom of the Self ($12.00)   _____

The Twelve Steps of Forgiveness ($10.00)   _____

The Circle of Atonement ($12.00)   _____

The Bridge to Reality ($12.00)   _____

From Ego to Self ($10.00)   _____

Virtues of the Way ($7.50)   _____

The Body of Truth ($7.50)   _____

Available Light ($10.00)   _____

Audio Tapes by Paul Ferrini

The Circle of Healing ($10.00) _____

Healing the Wounded Child ($10.00) _____

Forgiveness: The Original Blessing ($10.00) _____

The Poetry of the Soul ($10.00) _____

Seek First the Kingdom ($10.00) _____

Answering Our Own Call for Love ($10.00) _____

The Ecstatic Moment ($10.00) _____

Honoring Self and Other ($10.00) _____

Love Without Conditions ($19.95) 2 tapes _____

Ending the Betrayal of the Self ($16.95) 2 tapes _____

Relationships: Changing Past Patterns ($16.95) 2 tapes _____

Relationship As a Spiritual Path ($16.95) 2 tapes _____

Opening to Christ Consciousness ($16.95) 2 tapes _____

Posters and Notecards

Risen Christ Poster 11"x17" ($10.00) _____

Ecstatic Moment Poster 8.5"x11" ($5.00) _____

Risen Christ Notecards 8/pkg ($10.00) _____

Ecstatic Moment Notecards 8/pkg ($10.00) _____

Shipping

Priority Mail shipping for up to two items $3.95. _____

Add $1.00 for each additional item _____

Massachusetts residents please add 5% sales tax. _____

Add an extra $2.00 for shipping to Canada/Mexico _____

Add an extra $4.00 for shipping to Europe _____

Add an extra $6.00 for shipping to other countries _____

TOTAL _____

Send Order To: Heartways Press P. O. Box 99,
Greenfield, MA 01302-0099 413-774-9474
Toll free: 1-888-HARTWAY (Orders only)
www.paulferrini.com
www.heartwayspresss.com
email: heartway@crocker.com

Coming in 2002

A monumental work on sin and redemption
certain to become required reading in all Divinity Schools

ISBN 1-879159-48-1